The Spaces in Between

for Lynette

in all the ___ between

Orléans, 2003

The Spaces in Between

Selected Poems 1965-2001

STEPHEN SCOBIE

NeWEST PRESS

National Library of Canada Cataloguing in Publication Data

Scobie, Stephen, 1943-
The spaces in between

ISBN 1-896300-61-8

I. Title.
PS8587.C6A6 2003   C811'.54   C2003-910006-5
PR9199.3.S295A6 2003

Editor for the Press: Douglas Barbour
Cover photograph: "The spaces in between: Loch Monzievaird,
Perthshire, 1999" by Stephen Scobie
Cover and interior design: Ruth Linka
Author photograph: Evelyn Kreuzwieser

NeWest Press acknowledges the support of the Canada Council for the Arts and the Alberta Foundation for the Arts, and the Edmonton Arts Council for our publishing program. We also acknowledge the financial support of the Government of Canada through the Book Publishing Industry Development Program (BPIDP) for our publishing activities.

NeWest Press
201–8540–109 Street
Edmonton, Alberta T6G 1E6
(780) 432-9427
www.newestpress.com

1   2   3   4   5   06   05   04   03

PRINTED AND BOUND IN CANADA

for Maureen

as always

as everything

Contents

"Silvia, rimembri ancora . . ."
Giacomo Leopardi

"What thou lovest well remains"
Ezra Pound

Saint Andrews 1965

Sing low the new
the tender singing
Moonlight no more
crumbles on castles
or is brushed away
fingertip casualty
Here shall it stay
to its period of time
Here shall we say
the love words again
by the sand and sea

Leaving You My Best Farewell

Now you know your sinking sidewalk will not hold you—
the grey ship's sailed, the antique anchor fell.
When I'm gone, please remember what I told you—
that I'm leaving you my very best farewell.

In the morning when the dawn slides down to meet you
there are oceans tolling on your lighthouse bell—
but there's no need for their dragons to defeat you
once I've left you with my very best farewell.

There are special tables waiting for the heroes
in the taverns where you heard the sailors yell—
but I'll use red ink to mark your book with zeroes
if you won't listen to my best farewell.

When I found you, you were singing in God's heaven;
when I left you, you were beating time in hell—
but there surely are more angels than just seven
to interpret on their drums my best farewell.

If your sister with her monkeys still comes calling,
you could drown her in my Spanish wishing-well
and call out these words to her as she is falling:
Yes, he left me with his very best farewell.

Come to the bridge and wave to me on my freighter—
the grey ship's got abandoned love to sell.
The red whirlpool may come now or may come later,
but I've left you with my very best farewell.

The Black Ponies

They are gone, the black ponies—
desolate the city.

They were seen on one grey evening, people say,
upon the rooftops
prancing in precarious line. Since they have gone
the city is desolate, the horizon
empty. Yet citizens still gaze upwards
expecting what? Black ponies in a dancing line,
clattering the concrete ledges?

Black ponies in a dancing line,
clattering the concrete ledges.

One Word Poems

The word the wind speaks, coming in to land

trees

The word the boat speaks, making love to wind

sail

The word the cliff speaks, playing landlord

gannet

**The word the plough speaks,
white in the straight brown furrow**

gull

The word the rain speaks as it melts the snow

sorry

The metrical unit of the sea's vast poetry

wave

The spring's love song

Green(s)leaves

listen

listen

listen

silent

The Spaces In Between

Shoreline—a shifting space
between the land and sea, a tenuous
line, moving to some
equation.

      I love the things between—
like silences between two words:
not you, not me, but the love
between us.

      And in the café today
a friend explained how the Hopi Indians
based their numerical system on 8
because they counted, not their fingers,
but the spaces in between.

Naming Mountains

It must have been tough—
I mean, out West we've got
a lot of mountains. It took
some pretty fertile imaginations
to name them all. I think of
old explorers scratching their
heads, or wherever, and thinking
"What the heck can I call this one?"
Having run out of aunts,
uncles, sweethearts, passing
acquaintances, barmen, whores,
statesmen, animals, apt events,
moral abstractions, Indian names
(suggested by the guide), and still
saving up their own
names for a bigger one—
how many said "Mount
Horseshit!" and passed on,
out of the annals of
geography?

Made in USA / Jean-Luc Godard

Le bonheur, par example . . .

Here she lies with her dark hair spread over happiness. There is, for example, a book in her hands as she lies, perhaps on a bed. Alone. No, it is not in her hands; the book lies over her breast. Happiness is in her hands. She looks to her right. Her right hand holds a strand of her hair, which is spread over perhaps a pillow. A book lies over her breast. Her dress is happiness. The book is called *Adieu la vie, adieu l'amour.* Her eyes look into happiness. It is far away. Soon she will wear a trenchcoat; carry a gun. Her dress has a pattern of large squares: dark red, dark brown, dark yellow, dark happiness. Her dark hair spreads. Goodbye to life, goodbye to love, lies over her right breast. Her right hand holds a strand of dark hair spread. It is spread over where she is lying. A bed, for example, or happiness. Do you remember happiness? Just for example, long ago. There won't be any more, until the future. Here she lies with her dark hair spread over happiness; the book lies open on her breast. Her lover is dead. Her lover is dead and the search begins, always, here.

. . . oh David, tristesse.

Lenin at the Cabaret Voltaire

Lenin, when you sat there
did you listen, did you hear the
sounds they said?
were you only in
dark corners of your
vast mind plotting?
building nations?
bombs beneath your table?

Tzara, Ball, when you
spoke your poems there
did you see him
in his corner? did you
know he had a world to
blow up too? walls not of
art to tear down? and with
many ruins he would still be
scared of you?

Zürich, city of so
many languages what did
you hear? what silent
sounds? the rushing
Limmat dark and strong
between its walls and
under bridges from the
lake the Alps past all
your graceful spires oh
city?

Word Is

word is
to the kitchen gone, and
word is
to the hall

word is
in my mind, and
in my
understanding

word is
holding me
word is
my path
I will walk
in the ways
forever

word is
light before me
word is
dark behind me
word is
on my tongue, is
breath
and thought
word is
all my treasure

word is
playing
word is
praying
speech is
word
on word
is stone

word is
underneath, the
arms
word is
father
word is
found
word is
in my
generation
word is
holy
word is
found
is
found
is
found
is
found
is
found
is
word is
you
is
now
is
here
is
always

word without end
amen

The Corner of Abbey Street and Greenside Place

He was my friend and I listened when he told me
things I had never wanted to hear. And I said nothing
which was all he wanted me to say.

We drank from a bottle of wine until it was empty
and the gas-fire ran out its shilling. Then we went outside
and walked together in the wind.

Some silence grew in the middle of his words (he
never stopped talking), some silence we would never need to break,
some things we need never mention again. On the corner,

when we stopped outside the windows of their house,
the windows were dark. All these people we both loved so hopelessly,
behind their windows they all were sleeping.

Bridge-jumper

You thought you'd reached the end of the bridge;
we said it was only the middle, and you stepped off
to prove us right, to prove us wrong.

But what a place to dive from, die from,
out of the image and into the dream: song
of water in its solid form, rising to meet you
like the wall round every secret garden
you dreamed in your romantic youth.

It was the place I always waited for you: midnight
between the old year and the new: the point
where the cables' arc and the shallower curve of the bridgedeck
touch, meet for a moment, depart:
point of suspension, equation of grace, impossible meeting
of all such contraries as you and me. I had
been there before, in the wind, often: but never
jumped, or thought of jumping, into the black
chasm beneath us—being
proud of my height and the bridge's symmetry
stretching to each side equal
but yet to different shores. Not so for you:
what seemed the farther shore was only
the one you left behind on Friday.

So in your garden now you float alone, and the green
of plants is the green of water, the tides have swung you
out and through the Straits to ocean, all
the ungovernable passageways beyond that deadly wall.

Saturday Night

Saturday night was when my father worked:
no time of relaxation, the centre of his week.
He sat in his study, translating his beliefs
into the wise and simple words of his sermons.

Around 10.30 he might come downstairs,
drink tea, eat toast and marmalade, and watch
TV replays of the afternoon's games;
and then return to his desk and blue-covered notebooks.

For forty years he followed this good discipline:
and when he preached, the congregation listened
to the words of a friend they had known at times
when life did things they could not understand.

An hour or so ago I came home from a movie:
the house was quiet, the TV doesn't show Queen's Park.
I sit in my study thinking of my father,
writing this poem late on Saturday night.

My Grandmother's Name

My mother's mother's name: Garvie
from the Gaelic *garbh* meaning
rough and first

of all that name, was Ian
son of the Macleans of Coll,
a clansman of the Hebrides

who fought for the Stuart cause
in 1651 at Inverkeithing:
was wounded: and never went home.

He stayed behind in a foreign country (Scotland)
where few could speak his language:
yet from that language he chose a name
as if to defend himself:

a rough name, chiselled through centuries
into respectable merchants, ministers,
prosperity of the lowland line.
Then, after seven generations,

my mother's brother died
at war in a foreign country (France)
surrounded by a language of slaughter
no name could defend him from.

For Archie Fisher

Falkland was the royal hunting palace
—here the Queen rode out

and her wrist was wearing the wind
like a bracelet
                    like a hawk

You live here now
under the Lomond hills

the Queens all dead
except in your songs

Harlequin Acrobat

This ball I balance on is like the world
and I practise by the shores of the sea
where the tide rolls in from the edge of the world

My costume looks like a chessboard
whose buttons are kings and queens
which play for my heart until they fall
the threads unravelling

The shoreline shifts like a slack
highwire: the lock of hair
swept across my forehead like Picasso's
threatens my balance

Ignorant clown

There is a boat that comes to shore
a woman sitting in the stern
she holds a diary I wrote
in the years before I was born

And nothing whispers but the wind
(the rocks are screaming)
and nothing whispers but the wind

My name is the last in the catalogue
I balance on the edge of The End
my costume flies like a tattered flag
in mourning for this century

You come to me from Spain
and still the gun is in your hands
Applaud, applaud

Arlequin Acrobate

Sur ce ballon, comme sur le monde,
je me balance, m'exercant sur la plage
ou monte la marée du bout du monde

Ma chemise à carreaux, c'est un échiquier
dont les boutons sont des rois, des reines
qui jouent pour mon coeur avant de tomber
parce que la trame est fatiguée

La frange des vagues va et vient
comme la corde détendue du funambule:
sur mon front la mèche des cheveux,
celle de Picasso, me déséquilibre

Saltimbanque, tu ne sais rien

Voilà une barque qui s'approche du rivage:
à la poupe une femme assise
tient le journal que j'avais écrit
pendant mes années prénatales

Il n'y a que le vent qui siffle
(parmi les cris rauques des rochers)
il n'y a que le vent qui siffle

Je suis le dernier nom du catalogue
je me balance au-dessus de la Fin
ma vieille chemise vole en lambeaux
drapeau en berne pour ce siècle

Tu me viens d'Espagne
un fusil dans tes mains encore
Dis moi bravo: bravo, bravo

The Amateur

He perfected disguises,
but that did no good.
Lightning always
struck twice at his door.

Horizons tightened around
his rowing hand. His boat
drunk on remembrance
spun into darkness.

He thought of
Deptford, Marlowe's death;
longed for the dagger
slender in his brain.

Half-forgotten childhood toys
returned to whisper
the old accusation:
Amateur!

At last he found
after repeated failures
cold secret pleasure
in the phasing moon.

Black Circle

Lays the Black Spot on Billy Bones
image of his deadlight eye:
Blind Pew.
         Black circle,
circumference of a tapping stick, the hooves
beat in like thunder.

         Eyes spurred out,
Gloucester, searching for the cliff
his son denies him: finds it
within himself, sees his way clear
to destruction.

         Kip
in the whip's caress, with glory
burned into darkness, down:
sits quiet by a neighbour's fire—a child's
first cry, accusing, in his ears.

Black circle where these eyes are closed,
ears strain for song: blind
Homer drinking wine
and seeing the wine
dark sea.

Dumb Animals

"In the case of Jacques Ferron, who was taken in the act of
coition with a she-ass at Vanvres in 1750, and after due process
of law, sentenced to death, the animal was acquitted on the
grounds that she was the victim of violence and had not partici-
pated in her master's crime of her own free will. The prior of
the convent, who also performed the duties of parish priest, and
the principal inhabitants of the commune of Vanvres signed a
certificate stating that they had known the said she-ass for four
years, and that she had always shown herself to be virtuous and
well-behaved both at home and abroad and had never given
occasion of scandal to any one, and that therefore 'they were
willing to bear witness that she is in word and deed and in all her
habits of life a most honest creature.'"

E.P. Evans, *The Criminal Prosecution and Capital
Punishment of Animals* (London, 1906), p. 150.

For the ass it was no joke—those idiots
would kill her, would slit their sharp
steel into her throat, would close
her long ass-ears to all
the sounds they were saying. Reality
for her was nothing verbal: we have
no words that will even mean
how meaningless words were for her.

And for us it's no joke either—
when language goes mad, speech
schizophrenic, when meanings are glibly
bounced off words like balls from a bat—
somewhere incomprehensible knives
are being sharpened for us, and who can we

turn to for witness, who will say
and in what language, that you and I
have never given occasion for scandal
and are in all our habits of life as honest

as a she-ass being raped
under the ignorant sun?

The Children of Photographers

Hand on hip, against the wind-swept trees
(those confident flicks of Gainsborough's wrist)
the Blue Boy poses
                    unconvinced of his background.

Master Jonathan Butthall, given this mirror
into which (how many times?) he gazed
seeking the confirmation of that arrogant charm
which gave him immortality
                    (longevity at least)
on the lids of a million candy tins—

given this mirror, then, by parents
who could afford to pay: this one reflection,
solitary image of the vanished years
when he could turn his back on such a wilderness
and seek no mirror but his own brown eyes.

But we who are the children of photographers
inherit our images daily, watching them
develop in a safe red light.
Arranged in albums, framed by our bedsides,
the pictures of our age and youth surround us
shattering mirrors into kaleidoscopes
                    and catching us
forever glancing over our shoulders
afraid of the storm in the treetops.

The hand has left the hip now: we use it
to cover our eyes. We have seen ourselves too often
to believe in the security
of any image. Passports, driver's licenses, IDs.
Our eyes have grown hard

from gazing into cameras, cameras gazing back.

It would be more honest to photograph
only the backs of our heads
as we turn to face that confident
sketch of a storm.

West Side Story

My brothers were too much older, too
many years distant to teach me
essentials. They were always more expert
at golf or at chess, and they went to
romantic places like New York, or else to
Glasgow University. But Andy did show me
how to tie a Double Windsor knot, and also
he brought home the long-playing record
of *West Side Story*. It was the original
Broadway cast recording: I played it so often
I knew every word. One afternoon he attempted
to teach me theology: going over his notes
he used me as an audience, explaining
ideas to me to make them come clear
to himself. Too bad that when he began
I was listening to *West Side Story* and he didn't
cancel the record, just turned it down low, not
low enough: in the hiss of the needle
I was straining to follow the words, all the way
to the end of Side One:

> *One hand*
> *One heart . . .*

I finally saw it on stage, 1960,
King's Theatre Glasgow, an evening of fog,
all the buses delayed, I was sure I would miss
the curtain, but didn't. And later the film, time
after time, despite
the schmuck playing Tony, time
is twenty years ago and I always tie
my ties in Double Windsor knots, tonight

> *tonight, won't be just any night*

tonight the wind bites west of Broadway

hard in my face as I cross Times Square
coming out of the theatre, shaken to find
it is all still there, a classic, dated,
the audience as neutral as if it were truly
distant Verona, adolescents of Shakespeare:
familiar scenes, the choreography
of twenty years gone by, how old
would Maria be now? who would the Jets
have voted for in New Hampshire primaries?
walking up 7th Avenue, the porno theatres
blaring attractions of the midnight show
and Tony dead, Maria still alive
clutching a long black shawl, shuffling along
these west side sidewalks where the story
never ends

and later, writing down these lines to send
to Andy, who has never been
to the harsh excitement of New York City
or shivered as that west side wind
funnels through canyons of the streets,
who has never paused on a corner, waiting
to step out into traffic on the last
tentative intersection, 7th and 51st,
then in the hotel bedroom taking off
my tie with the Windsor knot—

the songs now locked in my head
repeating like sirens in the street below
the constant sirens of New York, drawing
their long sound out across the rivers
wailing all night outside my window
like sound effects offstage
as the final curtain falls.

NYC: February 26th, 1980

F an/atics

A student from Saskatchewan tells me
how much he adores Joni Mitchell
he'd like to write an essay on her but
is scared of being critical he
loves her too much: she comes home
each Christmas to see her parents he says
one year he and a friend camped out
in sleeping bags at Saskatoon airport
all through the holidays meeting each plane
in hopes to catch a glimpse of her

and as he talks I'm remembering

Mort at lunch one hour before
talking about his Auntie Babe, who had
a baseball autographed by Al Capone
and who lived just a couple of blocks away
from the Biograph cinema in Chicago
and ran with the rest when the news came through
that Dillinger was dead
lying shot in the street, and she still
holds onto the handkerchief
she dipped and took home
soaked in his blood

Songs on the Radio

here comes the night
here it comes
like a song on the radio

driving CHED, straightahead
down this suspicious highway
north and far:

listening once with Leisha
in front of the fire, the only
time I ever visited
her home in Irvine: her father
asleep in his chair oblivious
to her mad German mother
screaming: and nothing else
remains in memory

except for the song: Van Morrison
sang lead, with Them (the distanced
term of alienation) from
the North of Ireland, a raw
unfinished country, breaking
apart: a raw
unfinished emotion, night
"the long the long the lonely night"

and Leisha, whom I never quite
decided to be in love with, she
and I knew what it meant
sometimes in the dark
old streets of our city, our cold
and ancient city:
cold in her bones, she wrote me
once I had gone, once at a distance

of five thousand miles
I could admit I had loved her
far too late
for any good it might have done, here
comes the night
"the night the night the lonely night"

playing now on my car's radio
somewhere near Gibbons, Alberta
on Highway 37, heading north
with a fine snow falling
into my silent eyes

Someday Soon
(for Phyllis Webb)

"Someday Soon" is a song from the dark
evenings in Paris: the wintering sun
hidden above the fifth floor rooftops
without an elevator never made it down
to the room where we buried the daylight
inside the dismal orange of our walls.

The voice was Judy Collins, and the song
was the opening track on one of the few
records we played and re-played, our nostalgic
repertoire of memories: for even in Paris
that "old blue northern" blows across
the vacant prairie landscape of desire.

Tonight the Edmonton radio plays it again
as I leave a Grant MacEwan reading and drive across
the freeway to the flickering fires
of Refinery Row: "driving in tonight
from California," or in this case from
the sound of your voice, Phyllis, and your song:

considering suicide, that last and strange
walk along the rocky island shore,
confusion of the ocean with a home:
what does the eye take in of sea or sky
before it closes on the final blue,
leaving a life like letters at your door?

Two voices in the harmony of waves:
the salt waves springing on the fragile shore,
wavelength of radio lapping round my car
driving the memory, as songs always do,
to consider the poem of Paris, the poem of pain:
"Someday soon, going with him, someday soon."

The Wayward Wind

"Who remembers Gogi Grant?"
—*Playboy*, October 1978

Well I do, for one—
the wayward wind
in her thin nasal voice
cutting across
the years of my youth
on the record my brother
brought back from New York
with its words of the wind
and a wandering man
from a space so much wider
a sky far more open
than any I'd known
and a voice so much darker
so smoky and near
to the edge of a dream
I hadn't yet dreamed

Judy Garland

They used to set her songs so high
her voice had to reach and strain
as the anxious audience waited, waited

to see if she would snap and fall
so they could wrap her in their morbid love
and push her back on stage again, again

      (retreating each night to the fierce
      insomniac rooms crammed with noise
      the midnight telephone or blaring lights
      her children with their adult eyes
      greeting the strangers who knocked on her door
      with nightly packages of pills, of pills)

collapsing at intermission, tearing away
the sweat-soaked dress, disguising herself
in ice and perfumes: then sobbing, swearing,
heading back out to the stage, the stage

hand raised in supplication, or
to see if it was shaking: but her voice
beyond the limits that she knew
over the rainbow, making it through.

A Death in the Family

The clock on her sideboard still
shows summer time: she died
a week before winter.
                    Here we sit
nephew and grand-daughter
sifting through
                    photographs, papers
a death in the family.

                    Young
and handsome in uniform, direct eyes
disguising the trenches, this
was a man she loved. On the back
in her scrawly hand, with
no further comment: "Died in France,
1917."

        Here is the man she married,
trim moustache pointed: her cousin
over from Canada to fight
this war to end all wars. And here
is a postcard showing the bride-ship
which sailed war-brides to Canada, cargo
of peacetime promises.

                            She left her home
early in summer: by the end of the year
her mother had died of cancer. Letters
describing the death: "she went to sleep
like a tired child," reminding her husband
of a hymn at sunset. Also my father wrote
formally signing himself
"Your loving brother," 1922.

                    The years
on farms in Alberta: Whitecourt,
Athabasca. No letters survive.
One photograph shows her standing in snow
holding the skin of what may be
a wolf. More formal poses taken
at studios in Edmonton. Her children
toddling through gumbo. Farming or
trying to farm
Alberta in the 30s. No wonder no letters,
no diaries survive.

                    1937:
my father writes again. A death
in the family. Their father died
in January, harsh New Year.
"I sat with him several nights.
He did not speak. I think he knew me."
Why did she keep
these letters? Oh, there are also
wedding announcements, photographs
of brides and babies, clippings
of public events and celebrations—
                    but the letters
the letters she kept are all
about death. Forty years later she carefully preserved
my father's last letter before *he* died:
the generations, a continuity.

They abandoned Alberta in '38:
her husband swore he'd leave
if Aberhart got in, and he did.
Then lied about his age in 1940
to join the Reserves: she wrote
a poem in his honour: "Off
to fight the Hun." As it was

in France, 1917. Old soldiers fade—
as he did, finally, in '49. I never heard
her speak about him.

                    The photographs
show children, and a visit "home"
to Scotland in the 1950s (I remember
my childhood fascination for her curious
hooded eyes, and her extravagant alarm
about grass fires). She welcomed me when I came
to Canada in '65. Years in the wind,
years in the long slow North Vancouver rain.

She began to write
an autobiography, recalling
she was born at 8.20pm
on a Saturday evening, a most
inconvenient time in a manse:
remembers her father muttering
under his breath, rehearsing his sermons:
a cryptic note on the Boxer Rebellion:
how as a child she had longed
for a middle initial—five
lucid, beautiful pages
then stopped.

                    In 1972
my father died, and Jean, the middle sister,
in 1977. Oldest of three
and the last alive
she gathered her photographs;
wrote out family trees in a now
much shakier hand; neatly
labelled her letters; picked up the phone
to talk to a friend one morning and
between one sentence and another
died.

A week before winter, in
the North Vancouver rains, or in the long
sweep of wind over Athabasca.
Stirring her fine white hair.
Closing her hooded eyes.

November 4, 1979

Over Home

standing in this window
my father knew
he had come home

the hills to the west are lit
by sunshine after rain
they shine like glass, it seems
they could be broken

this house I never saw
my father at home in
every room

dying he told my mother
Don't worry
I'm still here

Cha Till Gu Brath

(1)

Even the walls of the room
have disappeared
where, Alastair, you sat
in the glow of the small gas fire
that measured time in shillings
snug from the snell east winds:

in Abbey Street the houses
we lived in are demolished:
like ghosts in mid-air
angles and corners jut
into vacant space:
where you sat is suspended
over a widened street:
the room itself is gone

through which your rambling conversation wove
patterns of time, Catullus
to *Catch-22*, the fortifications
of Berwick, and the tangle
in which our own unfortified
lives were mired, hurting like hell, that
winter of our discontent:

but hearing a song I remember still
your eyes with excitement gleaming
pedantic in your erudition
as you read me the Gaelic lament
and your own translation
suspecting how soon it would be
for us, and the time we shared:

Cha till   cha till   cha till MacCruimen
An cogadh no an sìth cha till e tuilleadh
Le airgiod no nì cha till MacCruimen
Cha till gu bràth   gu là na cruinne

No more   no more   no more MacCrimmon
In peace or war no more returning
For silver nor naught comes back MacCrimmon
No more at all   till the gathering day

(2)

So to the dead we say
nothing—
for they cannot hear

Words we carve for the living
onto stones, and they
become a city, become
a carving on our minds

        No more returning
        no more at all
        until the gathering day
        neither for silver nor for gold
        in peace or war no more returning
        neither to mountain nor to river
        to day nor night returns no shadow
        never again
        no more at all
        till the gathering day

Stones bear in silence
the pain of our carving:

the Cuillins form
a grey wall over water:
you also
shall reach the silent mountains

As the tides depart
from the rocks beneath Dunvegan
so departs MacCrimmon
As the tides return
to the red rocks of Dunvegan
so returns MacCrimmon
never
Nor can the moon tug him back
Nor can the waters
carry his music

Cha till gu bràth   gu là na cruinne

Munich: in the English Gardens

You remember me
walking past ruined buildings
carefully preserved
in the streets of Munich:
walking through the English Gardens.

I don't remember it at all:
not a case of forgetting, no
I insist
I never was there.

Amnesiac area: we are both
shut out
by the other's remembering.
The past is so fragile, so
dependent on our memories
agreeing with each other: all our life
together could disappear
as easily as smoke on the wind
when one of us says
"I don't remember. I never was there."

Sometimes you joke and say
it's like a psycho horror film
I'm trying to drive you crazy
denying what you know is true.
I smile and say reassuring
condescending things—which of course
is precisely what I would do
in the movie.
Other times I imagine you
walking through Munich alone
walking through the English Gardens

and I see myself beside you
the way I must always have been
those years before I knew you:
> the opposite of forgetting
> a shadow in no sunlight
> a ghost of the future
> a name on the tip of your tongue
> the opposite of memory

I'm walking with you through Munich
as you must have walked with me
all those years through St Andrews
all those dark lonely nights
I was never alone.

mooneow / sooneow
for Marilyn Buffalo MacDonald

first *mooneow* she ever saw
in the Devon Hotel
coming up from Hobbema
she remembers it still
aged three in the Devon Hotel
first city too
aged three coming up from Hobbema
the old Devon Hotel
demolished now
at the foot of MacDonald Hill

all evening
the cars coming down
going up that hill
white lights in front of them
red lights behind
so pretty
strung together like beads
aged three
all evening sitting at the window
of the old
Devon Hotel

time for bed, got to go to the bathroom
gets lost
                of course
aged three in the Devon Hotel
she opens a door
to the men's room
mooneow
first white man she's ever seen
stands shaving his face

has hair all over
long curly hair on his neck
moustache above
a beard of white foam
hair on his chest
white skin
hair curling on his toes
barefoot
none of the People
has so much hair
or such strange skin

she screams
coming up from Hobbema
remembers it still
aged three in the Devon Hotel
everyone comes running
the manager is mad
her parents get into trouble
all evening
watching the cars
white beads, red beads
on the string of MacDonald Hill

and remembers it now
telling the story
to a table of
white men, rich men
to show what she means by *mooneow*
white man
with moustache
and lots of hair
and lots of money

mooneow / sooneow
white man / money
there is nothing
accidental in rhymes

Forgetting (l'oubli)

The moment of forgetting
is like
the moment of falling asleep:
you don't
notice it: one
moment you could if you tried remember
the face
the detail, the
next you forget: one
moment you are if you think it awake, the
next you're asleep:
but you don't
notice it happening, if
you notice it it doesn't happen:
being awake you stay awake
remembering you don't forget.

Western Landscapes

Western landscapes: the prairie, the wayward
wind, the long line of horizon, smudged
when dust begins to rise: it takes
will power, stubborn determination,
thousands of back-breaking hours, and still those winds
blow fields and livelihood away, it is
the drought, the depression, all over again:
small crops and smaller harvests, praying for
rain before it's too late, before everything tumbles
down: the house, the mortgage, the barn, rattling like an old tin
can kicked down the highway, all for lack of
rain, oh sweetly suffering
Christ, of rain.
If this is the promised land, the last best west,
my outhouse is the Ritz. There isn't much to
love out here, remembering how things
were and will be again: you just have to dig yourself
in, into the soil, into the land, into the history,
my friend, the goddamn history: Riel taking up
arms, and Aberhart taking up votes,
and Lougheed now doing what
I don't know, it never ends, out here
in the West there's always a desperation, and
my heart goes out to it, down to it, oil and stone,
bed-rock, soil, the dust-devils blowing
again, in the 80s, again.

Molly

yes to arms
a that leg
and fourpence had
and help suits

suppose I cover and
there smelling coats like nothing
the hospital   it next
him much when bleeds

off party stack at bedroom
dying looked father
he blood   what   all appetite
of down pack meet

let married my what
time all for its picked
because a show me
be somebody

get now like hide before
have that bottom painted
getting his tending
them posing please and please

The Love Song of Alice B. Toklas

Alice knitted. I never did.
I never grew lonely.
Alice said something.
Alice never died.
Alice could outlast unruly servants.
I needled Alice sometimes.
Paris elicits cultural tension.
Alice could loosen everything.
Alice never died.
No orator tricked her.
I never greeted strangers.
Tomorrow regrets Alice.
No guide excelled Alice.
Sometimes I needled guides.
Let each history unfold
regularly, transitively.
Can opposites love
opposite roses?
Alice never died.
Alice negated Alice.
Roses repeated.
Alice never grumbled.
Every minute, each new time.
I needled Alice sometimes.
Yes, sometimes.
Times.
Every minute turns,
outlasting Parisian orators.
I never tired.
I never greeted.
Alice loosened love.
Take heart, I said.
Alice never died.

No orator tried.
Orators rarely die.
I needled Alice rarely.
Yes, needled.
Orators take unlimited needling.
Orators rarely die.
Early rose, easy death.
I never negated.
Orators twist roses.
Every second, every minute
Basket loved.
I never guided.
Take heart each day.
I felt feeling.
Every rose, every needle
can explain.
I said something.
Paris. Rose. Eternity.
Alice died.
I never grew.

Rain

Apollinaire let it fall on his page
drizzling the letters in columns down
across the white like a window pane
(or spell it "pain," pretend they're tears)
watching them splash on the Paris streets
and puddle into words. The rain
is also the language the West Coast speaks
surrounding us in a syntax of downpour
with sinuous long sentences of shore,
interjections of islands, rock and pine
tumbling like paragraphs
into the sea. It is the falling element
of shallow breathing: water in air
seeking its level, running to rivers,
climbing to clouds.
Blown by the wind it beats into your face
but do not bow your head: throat back
and open, drink the downpour down, let it stream
through sodden hair to streak like tears
(or spell it "pane," pretend you're glass)
across the cheekbones' watershed
to drop into your mouth like words
or evening letters, elements of breath,
the raindrops of a poem's dancing line
lit by the streetlamps along St. Germain,
let fall on pages by Apollinaire.

This Letter in My Father's Hand

This letter in my father's hand
completes full circle—

    my father wrote it, to
    his sister in wartime BC
    just four days after
    I was born—"rather small
    but with a very deliberate
    nose!"—my first review;

    and now my cousin moving house
    returns the text to its topic:
    my father's flowing, kindly hand
    in which I have not read any new words
    in ten years since he died

    touches me now with the news
    I am born, my existence is written
    across an ocean that could not be crossed
    in 1944, in words of war

—now leaving home I make a copy
(the writing doubled again)
to carry with me transAtlantic
to read to my mother the words
announcing this life she gave me

in the xerox
of my dead father's
loving hand.

May 1982

Poem beginning with the line
"Gertrude Stein didn't have a cat"

Gertrude Stein didn't have a cat.
She had a dog called Basket.
A cat would have been too inscrutable for Gertrude Stein.
She liked to know what people were thinking.
Basket only thought about Gertrude and Alice.
Basket only thought adoration.
That suited Gertrude Stein just fine.
She liked her admirers to be scrutable.
She always knew what Picasso was thinking.
Often he thought about the Katzenjammer Kids.
Georges Braque never thought about the Katzenjammer Kids.
Georges Braque was like a cat, endless and subtle.
Gertrude Stein didn't have a cat.

Cranach

When Cranach was 74 years old
he painted his vision of the Spring
of Eternal Youth.

        Old women arrive
in wheelbarrows and carts, out of
a landscape of stone:
they enter the pool with withered breasts,
old bodies bent in lamentation:
then suddenly are young again,
lovely and nude: a courtly gentleman
ushers them thoughtfully into a tent
from which they emerge in fine silk robes
to flirt behind bushes, eat at a banquet
laid out under the flourishing trees,
dance to the music of flutes and drum.

But as the legend has it, only women
profit from this transformation,
these waters working by the power of love:
their pleasant company and conversation
is all it takes to keep those courtly men
forever young: that is, those men
already on the far side of the pool; while back
on the other side, in the landscape of stone,
the old men carry women on their shoulders, staggering
towards the spring which will not work for them

—as Cranach noted, painting the scene
when he was 74 years old.

Gemäldegalerie, Dahlem, West Berlin, 1982.

Picasso's Radio

Picasso's radio played music
that no one else had even heard yet.
Sitting in Paris in 1911
he was already listening to Bob Dylan.
He knew The Rolling Stones by heart.
He would say to Georges Braque, "Georges,
there's this really neat group called The Eagles,"
but Braque was busy playing Bach
on classical clarinet. "Gertrude," Pablo would say,
"you'd love this record called *Blonde on Blonde*,"
but Stein would give him a stony stare
and turn a deaf ear. So Picasso would go
back to his studio there in the Bateau Lavoir
and turn up *Beggars' Banquet* loud, until Juan Gris
banged on the ceiling. Alas, when he moved
to bourgeois quarters in Montparnasse,
Picasso left his radio behind. He always wanted
to find it again, to tune in to Tina Turner,
but some unscrupulous second-hand dealer
has hoarded it away in his basement
where every night he listens to paintings
the world will never see.

In Memoriam, Warren Zevon, "Mohammed's Radio."

The Correction Line

                          zigs and then zags
setting the road to rights, and to right

angles: ninety degrees against the curve
of the wide flat earth, the invisible flaw

in all man's neat geometry. A line
extended to infinity goes wrong; two lines

will meet at the horizon, vanishing point
on the prairie's minimal canvas; both

extensions of the visible, into blind faith
in all you cannot know from here, this corner

where the road that once seemed endless stops
and, meeting no obstacle, turns in its tracks.

for Franz Stanzel

Interstate Seattle (I5)

Driving down into America, I'm driving
down into America. down. into. O

my America, my new-found-land
of insistent ahistoricity

where seasons are not called autumn or spring
but baseball and football, yr basic

driving downfield to the goal-line stand, it's
third and ten, the quarterback rolls out

into the flat, into the mid-West plains,
his pass on the thinnest ribbon of road

floats, into the tangle of traffic, freeways,
interception of a head-on crash

and the howl of sirens, cops with guns
hanging by their sides like handkerchiefs

stuffed into their pockets, referees' flags
fall on the play, an interference call

and with slow-motion replays the men on TV
agree it was a good call, a close call

so now it's first and goal, the fullback puts
his head down and bulls through, they need

tow-trucks to clear the wreckage, and cars
are backed up on the interstate for miles

clear to the Canadian border.

Lorele/i

My body passes on
a long trajectory of trains

stretched without comfort across
the angles of a corner seat

remembers, in the aches of certain muscles,
the trains I have asked it to sleep on

the years of crossing midnight countries
to dawn in a dingy terminus:

my body slowly going wrong
as it wears to its measuring halt

is still the site in which I name myself
the one who travels, rider on the rails

as they converge, criss-cross, lead back
to all the signs inscribing what "I" am:

my passport number, the book in my hand (on
authorship), the grey in my hair, the cut

of clothes I wear, and now the insistent lines
of a song "aus alten Zeiten" that comes

not mir-ly "aus dem Sinn" to this train's window
from Bonn to Koblenz, where "ruhig fliesst der Rhein"

while the sun on the opposite bank
"funkelt," yes, precisely, "der Gipfel des Berges

funkelt / im Abendsonnenschein," *ein*——
one, singular, I. Hein-e. Heinr-ich. Ich——

the space of these trajectories, the well-trained hand
that will sign my name to the foot of this page: *ich*

weiss nicht was soll es bedeuten, I
haven't the faintest idea what it means.

Housekeeping

There are days, days when it all comes together:
the signs of a journey, memory, the insistent trace
of all our synchronicities. This time it was in Stockholm:
late on a Wednesday night, after Doug and I
had spent the clouded February day
on trains across Sweden: leaving the sea
at Göteborg in the craning dawn, through trees
and deepening snows, to Katrineholm: change trains
and south to Linköping, a reading to give,
then back on the train: the woods like Alberta
scattered, sparse, and only the red oxide paint
as Sweden's signature on houses and barns.
And Doug was reading Marilynne Robinson
in between chapters of Derrida, but finding
Derrida everywhere: "relic, remnant, margin,
residue, memento, bequest, memory,
thought, track, or trace": and as he reached
the final pages, I was forced
to lay down my book (mere
Lawrence Durrell) and follow in
my memory, my trace, his reading of
the final pages, the bridge's crossing,
Sylvie and Ruth in the Swedish woods, each
page he turned, in the long
darkening night as our train reached Stockholm.
Then it was business as usual: find our hotel
and a place to eat—smoked reindeer meat
in a gloomy restaurant—and almost at midnight
we're trudging ankle-deep in city slush
back to our beds, when we pass a music store
still open at this hour, and packed with noise: the Swedish
kids in their Mohawk haircuts, leather
backs adorned with aggressive decals

of heavy metal groups: and here in Stockholm the latest
music from LA or Birmingham
blares out to the snow, and draws us in
to look and listen. Then the record changed
and I couldn't believe it, a song
from 61? or 62? John Leyton wailing
his only hit—"Johnnie Remember Me"—it meant
nothing to Doug, must have been only
a British success—so who in Stockholm at midnight
remembered him, the way he asked, but me, from the three
weeks or so that it lived in my head, in
Oban was it? one summer, so many
summers ago. So singing along I

> *see her in the sign*
> *of the wind sighin'*
> *in the tree tops*
> *way above me*

at the end of the long day's transit, nothing left
but go back to my room and write it down
still humming the tune, here in my diary:

> relic, remnant, margin,
> residue, memento, bequest, memory,
> thought, track, trace.

Fulford Harbour

for Phyllis Webb

The movement of tides, and more
insistent, the ferry's diurnal
restitching of wake, the full
fording of this harbour, in
and out, like needles of desire,
tiding, pulsing, engines' beat
vibrating even this house's
far foundations on
Morningside Road: the gleam
of white between the screen of leaves
outside the window, moving left
to right, like writing, reading, and
redrawn the other way, against
the flow, revision, retrospect:
lifting my head from a book
into this trope of repetition
beyond the pleasure principle, fort/
da, fort/da, full/ford, harb/
our lady of the changing tides
da/me de la mer, de la marée,
ferry-god/mother, mère, "mere
matter" (as you wrote, before
this window), turned again
into the move meant always to return.

The Disciple's Consciousness
: for Jacques Derrida,
on the death of Michel Foucault
Toronto, June 25th, 1984

(1)
And yes he said, yes yes, the double
performative of language, yes he said while
all of us said no, no to the death un-
timely announced, yes to the no he is dead,
yes to the man whose white head bowed is
waiting to speak again. Beginning again
at the source it is ours to nominate and sign:
the name at the end of the book, yes yes, I aye
will (in that other language) will to the end
of where we begin. He is walking alone
and seems small, the blue bag hanging from his shoulder,
with no words now to listen to, to give
an answer to the call. For if this seems an
empty conclusion, he said, there are times when we must be
very patient with emptiness. Yes. He said that.

(2)
This time, for me. While Angela is
crying, beside me, too many dead, that is
the age we've come to. Imagine. And here in Toronto
I've been thinking of Sharon Stevenson,
buying her book, re-
living her death.
There is no consolation in philosophy.
Only the sun. Only the love of wisdom,
which is woman. Take away my categories.

(3)
Only the sun and its reversal. Soleil noir.
And if wisdom is a woman, then
those who seek her will be male and will
be mused. The figure of the hierarchy, or
sitting at the master's feet. Breaking away
> "the disciple's consciousness, when he starts,
> I would not say to dispute, but to engage
> in dialogue with the master or, better,
> to articulate the interminable and silent
> dialogue which made him into a disciple—
> this . . . is an unhappy consciousness"
yes I say no, this time, to you. At the table
where the white sun only this morning
haloed his head. And he said farewell
for all time, for us all. Imagine.

Shepherds Abiding

But nobody says what the shepherds did *next:*
going back in the stiff cold dawn to their flocks,
or trying to get some sleep, with heaven's fire
still burning in their eyes: or after that
how long they held on to that memory crumbling
like sand through an hourglass, through tedious years
of scratching a living on Bethlehem's hills,
poor pastures, and the market for mutton falling:

that memory, for which no words were ever
quite simple enough, of a skeletal night
so cold that no one could sleep, and there they were
minding their sheep and their own business, when
the blaze of light came on them; in a daze
they found themselves down on their knees, in worship
of some poor homeless new-born boy and his
puzzled parents.

What they remembered more
was when the soldiers came, a week or so later,
and all these babies casually slaughtered,
their own among them, with sword and fire
and not an angel in sight to lift a wing
to save them.

Thirty years later,
if any surviving heard the Jerusalem news,
another wandering preacher who'd gone too far
and then a crew of fishermen babbling
of death and resurrection, these shepherds might have paused
to wonder about fishers so far from their boats—
and whether these men too might not be driven by
that same dissatisfaction of desire

that for so long made mere sheep-herding seem
out on the margins of the real world
of infanticide and absent angels.

Fisherman's Angel

Angel of mercy, angel
on the banks of the real river,
fisherman's angel, angel setting out
on a morning tide to the Isle of May,
angel of crow-stepped gables,
cave of the hermit under the cliff,
angel of shipwrecks and drowning sailors,
angel of the silver herring crans,
old drunken Scottish angel—
you will not let me go.

Pull me again out onto the margins,
stand with me by the edges of tide
and watch that scribbled line as it strays
back and forth to the tug of the moon.
Littoral or literal:
the moon is a wee Scots tugboat, nosing
the ocean liners of the earth
into their harbours:
Crail, Anstruther, Pittenweem,
the silver margin of the hem of gold
with its fields scrubbed clean and its waters
scudding under rainclouds driven in
by that old wind, cold wind, east wind,
whetstone of those rugged faces, snell
that never learned to turn inland.

Angel, where will you take me now
into the breath of light
that breaks from the clouds above the May—
the pathway of light that always leads
Christlike across the waters, always
straight to the sun?

If I walk that way, who cannot swim,
will your wings support me?
Or do you struggle too, sometimes,
is it hard to fly
forever with bedraggled feathers
on the falling currents of air
that shatter like glass beneath
your feet, and mine?
Angel, you're eighty years old
and your poor poets, middle-aged evangelists,
ease into the circuit of their sagging skin
each morning a touch more slowly
resenting the alarm.

It's time again for me to travel:
I'll buy another airline ticket,
I'll fly wherever you want me to,
I'll pass through security
taking my chances with bombs, or with
tickets that show no destination,
luggage that arrives on time
without a passenger to claim it
circling the baggage carousel
forever beneath the stars.
Angel, this trip's on me:
you'll be my travelling companion,
sit in the empty seat beside me,
lean over my lap to look out
at mountains of ice
and prairies of the sunlit clouds.
Angel, I promise you a good window view.
Angel, I promise to take you home.

Remains

A gate is banging in the wind
of 3 AM. Turn over in your
sleep. In your dream you were
in New York, you had to leave,
you were delaying your depar-
ture. As long as you kept on
writing you didn't have to go.
So you kept on writing: "A
gate is banging in the wind of
3 AM."

In the spring you come upon the Hanged
Man, suspended from an arbutus tree. One
leg is tucked behind the other in a figure 4.
He is swaying back and forth in the breeze,
and humming to himself, apparently quite
happily. The tune he hums is "I Heard It On
the Grapevine."

You have no right to remain
silent. You have no right to
speak against the state. We
shall choose your music for
you; we shall allow you to say:
I am guilty. This is the new
justice. This is the new mercy.

Oh Lord, this song is longer than my life. I
wanted to lay down this old guitar, I wanted
my voice to rest from the choruses. But what

can you do when you're spotlit in front of an audience, rinsing in your mouth the Law and the Prophets, holding in your hands the bloody stones of Jerusalem?

Tilting at windmills, you said, looking around for some windmills to tilt at. But you were caught in the Cariboo, the hillsides too steep for your old nag to tackle. So where does that leave you, Don Coyote?

Hermit, used as a verb, meaning: to wait, invisible, at the mouth of a cave. As in: she used to hermit all day on the shore near Tofino.

You look at the word pencilled, graffito, eye-level on the washroom wall. The single word "trout." Fictions of motivation form around it. Your own hand reaches towards a pen and pauses above it, waiting, like a hook.

To understand Derrida's idea of linguistic deferral, just think about your credit card limit. Think about it a long time. Try to imagine who the Master really is.

I saw you at the edge of the
storm, gathering broken
branches of pine from the
road. You were running before
the wind, your arms overflow-
ing, more branches down than
you could save or hold. All
night in my arms you smelled
like an orphaned forest.

Manic, he had bought eight telephones, and
then two answering machines to record their
messages. But nobody called. How could
they? There was no line into his house.

You got mixed up with your
pills, didn't you, you silly
bugger. You took just one or
many too many, went to sleep
in your chair, and never woke
up. For the first time in your
life, old friend, you were left
with nothing to say.

Berlin

The second city to be taken.

A city of spies and checkpoints, a city of shadows and treachery. The very streets seem ambiguous, sliding into unsuspected culs-de-sac, running into those guarded Walls between the heroes and their knowledge of themselves. For the spy, at the final accounting, Berlin is a state of mind; all the novels are psychomachia—their conflicts internal, their betrayals internal, their sad and musty deaths a death of the soul.

The toughest audience in Europe, Leonard says.

What I remember of Berlin in the early 1980s is a side-street under an S-Bahn line; tall and distinguished buildings whose walls still bore the scars of artillery; a tree-lined square I walked through every morning, with a tiny café at its corner, no more than three tables, and a group of old men who sat there drinking beer and watched me as I passed. The newspapers were full of Fassbinder's death, hinting at some secret connection to the death of Romy Schneider. On the empty ground before the ruined Reichstag, boys were playing football.

Berlin is the ghost that inhabits every other city. Above it, in the divided sky, Wim Wenders saw the angels hovering.

Border

The first time I saw the East German border was in 1963. I was on a student exchange to Göttingen, and our hosts took us, on a rainy Sunday afternoon, to see the wire. Some of them were East German refugees; I was in love with a woman called Heike (pale, remote, fragile), who had crossed in Berlin just a week before the Wall went up. Göttingen had signs everywhere: "Unteilbares Deutschland," Germany indivisible. But it had been divided, and the hurt was still raw.

I had expected the barbed wire; I had expected the guard-towers; I had expected the guns. I had not expected that strip of ploughed land between the fences, like a bitter parody of peaceful fields, a line of open soil that ran from north to south the length of Europe. On the far side, beyond the wire, a woman was standing under a red umbrella; close to us, a family was waving to her. She did not wave back.

The first time that I crossed it was in 1982, Berlin, a controlled tourist trip. The bus through Checkpoint Charlie. The long-handled mirrors checking under every vehicle. The empty spaces of the Russian War Memorial. The cold grey water of the Spree.

Then suddenly it's Lübeck, November 1989. The signs are the same: "Da drüben ist auch Deutschland." Over there it is also Germany. But now the wire is coming down. The guards are smiling, posing for photographs. The East Germans are selling their patrol dogs ("Mauerhunden," wall-hounds) for $35 each. In the city of Lübeck, this late November Sunday is like Carnival, the streets thronged. Third weekend now they're coming over, to gawk at the marzipan in Niederehe's windows. The raucous sounds of the Trabant engines cough among Opels and Mercedes like a crow in an exaltation of larks.

I stand there on the street that they used to call "the end of the world." For a moment I think I am standing under a red umbrella, looking back, over 26 years, at someone waving to me from the other side.

David Livingstone

He is the one who was found, although he was not lost.

It was the others who had lost him: the Victorian Missionary Societies at their afternoon teas, who sat on gracious lawns in England and plotted the boundaries of Empire. He was lost to them, all right. He had taken his stubborn Scottish morality out of the mills of Blantyre and set it loose in the African jungles, saying to all the God-fearing slavers: "Enough—these men are free." And then he went deeper in, the explorer, looking for a famous waterfall, looking for the source of Nile, looking for a living stone.

So they sent Stanley after him, believing he was lost; and Stanley, believing he had found him, found also the legendary words to say: "Dr. Livingstone, I presume?"

And like a fool (a polite, Presbyterian fool), David said Yes. And was lost.

Mirror

How do vampires comb their hair, I wonder? And when they floss their fangs in the morning, before retiring to their comfy coffins, what do they see in the bathroom mirror—only a foam of toothpaste, floating over vacancy?

If the mirror tells the truth, it does so always in reverse. The vampire sees his own true absence reflected; the rest of us see our sinister ghosts, our left-handed complements.

The first book of poetry I published, along with two student friends, was called *The Invisible Mirror*. One of us used a pseudonym. One of us is dead now.

I can never pronounce it properly; my teeth are in the wrong position for all those Rs. I take comfort in the fact that Bob Dylan can't pronounce it either; in his songs, it always comes out as "mere." It rhymes with "fear," with "clear," with "Johanna's not here."

Mere matter, mirror matter. Some people believe that there is a mirror-world, the negative of this one. We can slip into it in dreams, or pass through mirrors as thick as mercury. In that other world, none of us used a pseudonym. None of us is dead now.

Mirrors, we said in our epigraph, quoting Cocteau, mirrors would do better to reflect further.

Mona Lisa

She must have had the highway blues, the song says: you can tell by the way she smiles. Everyone can tell. Everyone knows that smile, or thinks they know that smile. It's a knowing smile. She sees the rocks behind her (she has eyes in the back of her head), and she's eager to truck on out of here, down the highway once more, just as soon as this fancy Italian gent has laid his brushes down.

"Draw me the Mona Lisa," a Frenchman asked me once. I was sitting at my favourite café in St. Germain, and we'd struck up a conversation along the normal lines of I'm not an American, I'm a Canadian. "Everyone," he insisted, "has an image of La Gioconda; draw yours for me"—and he pushed a paper napkin across the table of the Bonaparte. I tried a crude sketch of a smiling face and crossed it out; attempted it instead in words. "Mon 'a' lit ça," I wrote, and offered it to him. A Canadian pun! He was delighted.

Mon 'a' lit ça. My 'A' reads that. The letters getting started, getting started to smile. She is reading the painter's face, and the movements of his hand. Through her Louvre shield of bulletproof glass, she is watching the world watching her. She is still eager to leave, but just for the moment something holds her here, at the beginning of her alphabet. She already knows what I have written on this page: you can tell that by the way she smiles.

Oedipus

Here he comes limping.

Swollen foot, cripple, here he comes, limping into the twentieth century. "Hey mister," people shout at him, "you sure walk funny."

He reaches the place where three roads meet.

"Get out of my way," he says to the man who is standing there, nursing his cancerous jaw. "Get out of my way or I'll kill you."

"You can't kill me, I'm dead already," the man explains, reasonably enough. "I am the ghost of Sigmund Freud."

"I'll kill you anyway," says Oedipus. And he does—just like so many times before.

Then he limps off, in the general direction of Thebes.

Rain

The loneliest kind of weather. Even when there's singing in the rain, it's never a choir. People who walk in the rain like to do so by themselves, hunched into trench-coats with the collars turned up, eyes on the ground watching for puddles. In *films noirs*, the night streets glisten with rain, and Robert Mitchum or Ida Lupino walk into it, backs to the camera, as if it were the baptism and blessing of their dark obsessions. "After a while," says Hemingway's hero at the end of *A Farewell to Arms*, after Catherine has died, "I left the hospital and walked back to the hotel in the rain."

Rhymes with cocaine. And so is everywhere in Dylan: expecting rain, lost in the rain in Juarez, Louise holds her handful of rain. . . . Rhymes with pain. Rhymes with Pontchartrain. Rhymes, in the end, with just about anything you want it to.

Telephone

People in movies are always saying, "I can't talk about this on the telephone." *Why not?* Even when, in the plot, they have no earthly reason to suppose that their phones might be tapped, they still "can't talk about it on the phone." Is it just the scriptwriter trying to drum up suspense? Or is there some taboo, we all instinctively feel, about what you can *say* to someone you can't *see*?

The telephone puts the voice at a distance: the speaker is in your ear and yet not present. Somewhere along its electric translation, speech becomes writing. The wires get crossed; misconnections multiply. All numbers are wrong numbers. The line is busy.

Or as the British say: the line is engaged. The line has made a promise of marriage: it links you, across its distances, to the Other who hears. This promise is never more than a fingertip away. Lift up the phone and say Hello? Who is this? When you hear the beep, marry me.

Postscript:

The cellphone transforms all these observations, all these eavesdroppings. It takes everyone out of their private cells; no one is any longer imprisoned. We hear it all: on trains, on streetcorners, in cafés. We speak in private in public. The answer to our most personal needs must always be Yes.

Horn OK Please

It is when you land in Bombay
and your suitcase has landed in Singapore, and three days
later in Ahmedabad you are trying to explain to a customs
official why no one at midnight at the airport would give you
an importation certificate for a suitcase you didn't have, and
the suitcase arrives looking so battered and covered in labels
and felt-pen hieroglyphics that for a moment you don't
recognise it as your own, and you sit there wondering
whether this would take longer or shorter if you offered some
discreet baksheesh as the customs officials express great inter-
est in your seven reels of blank videotape, and after sixteen
triplicate forms you step out slightly dazed into the sunshine
with a change of underwear at last

It is when Rakesh invites you home
and you climb three storeys in the shabby apartment building
facing the oil refinery, and sit on the low bed over the stone
floor in the dark room which is cool even in the heat of the
day, and drink a bottle of sickly sweet pop called Thums Up,
and his mother sits silently beneath the television set and
some faded family photographs, and his 2-year-old sister
plays on the floor with the pages of The Times of India in
which the headline records that Australia's bowling has blown
India's batting "asunder"

It is when the motor rickshaw driver
pulls into the side of the road with smoke pouring out of the
tiny engine beneath his seat, and in his two or three words of
English says something about pistons and asks if you speak
any Gujarati, and drives a hundred metres down the road and
stops again with the engine making ever more terrible noises,
but refuses to call you another rickshaw because after all you
are his fare and he has promised on his honour to take you to

the Gandhi Ashram, and when you get there finally, his
engine wrecked beyond repair, Vara disputes what he's charg-
ing you and beats him down from twelve rupees to eleven

It is when the taxi driver late at night
confesses he has no idea where he is going, and stops to ask
for directions on a dark road in a city where some sections
are cordoned off because of religious riots, and a crowd
comes out of the darkness and stands round the taxi and
peers in at you with friendly curiosity and says "Where are
you coming from? You are coming from Canada? That is
very good," and when at last you get back to the guesthouse he
asks for a hundred rupees and you pay it without question,
feeling guilty about Vara

It is when Rani takes you to the bazaar
and you sit on the carpets in a shop no larger than a double
bed which nevertheless has an infinitely expandable supply of
scarves and saris and tablecloths and cushion covers and
embroidered jackets and extravaganzas in silk and sequins,
and no matter what you see or say you like there is always one
more length of gorgeous fabric to be unfolded and laid at
your feet, while you marvel at exchange rates and worry about
the capacity of your by this time famous suitcase, and some-
one comes in with cups of masala tea, and Rani smiles and
invites you to her home too

It is when you look at the cows
which are wandering through the city streets looking as peace-
ful as the blissed out animals in a Franz Marc painting, and
which seem as far as you can tell to be grazing on nothing at
all but dust and crumbling concrete, and you hear all around
you the din of an Indian city, the trucks roaring past with the
signs on the back of them reading Horn OK Please, and a
thousand people are honking their horns OK to please the
truck drivers, and Nita beside you is earnestly asking what you

think is the current condition of postmodernism in
Canadian poetry

It is when you are standing in line
     to get through emigration at Bombay airport at 3 AM with
     several hundred angry American tourists whose plane was
     supposed to leave half an hour ago, and a woman who says
     she's a travel agent is muttering about the Warsaw conventions
     and threatening to sue Lufthansa, and you're feeling cau-
     tiously smug since you're travelling by Cathay Pacific, and you
     discover that the couple behind you in the line live two blocks
     away from you in Victoria and the dentist they go to is the
     man who sold you your house, and after another two and a
     half hot hours in a dingy departure hall you're finally on
     board and can see dropping away beneath you the lights of
     Bombay and the great darkness of its slums

that's when you know that you're lost
     and unlike your suitcase
     you're never going home

The Eyelash of a Camel

"Look closely," he said, and handed me a magnifying glass. I was in a crafts shop in Agra, one of those inevitable stops on any taxi-driver's route, and this very smooth, very well-spoken salesman wanted me to inspect a 17th century painting on silk. It showed the dynasty of Shah Jahan, the builder of the Taj Mahal, and Mumtaz, the dead wife for whom he built it. Their faces, and those of their ancestors and descendants, were inlaid around a picture of the Taj itself. Even to the naked eye, the painting was finely precise and meticulous; enlarged in the glass, the details were even more detailed. What had seemed to be mere lines became fully rendered bodies, walking in the gardens. Yet even enlarged, there was no hint, no trace, no betrayal of anything so coarse as a brush-stroke. The urbane salesman explained: the brush would have consisted of a single bristle. The eyelash of a camel.

Can the eyelash of a camel enter the eye of a needle?

Consider Shah Jahan, a rich man entering paradise. Each evening, he sits on his throne before the reflecting pool, he watches the light as it crumbles into the marble of the Taj. In twilight, the Taj Mahal fades into the sky; the marble takes on the colours of the atmosphere; the massive dome becomes insubstantial; it floats, it rises into the air. The tomb of Mumtaz enters paradise, through the eyelash of a camel. And darkness falls, complete at last, over Shah Jahan.

He is in the Red Fort. He is his own son's prisoner. Along the sweeping bend of the river, he can see a side view of the Taj Mahal. He can no longer see its reflection in the pool, but he sees its reflection in his mind, in the empty space on the facing bank, where he had planned its unbuilt double. His own tomb: the Black Taj, inverse mirror. The love and death of Mumtaz answered, finally, by the death and love of Shah Jahan. What remains, now, is this triangulation of desire: the White Taj glowing in the sunshine; the Black Taj existing in negative space; and the Red Fort.

The salesman is entering paradise. "A single bristle," he tells me. "The eyelash of a camel." He locks the painting away in the Red Fort of its showcase. Somewhat to my surprise, he does not try to sell me anything.

Queen Mary, She's My Friend

The question includes its own
answer: in my beginning is
my end. Remember Queen Mary, making
friends with the headsman's axe. What
is the end? All of her future days,
blowing like smoke from a casual fire
in the forest of her heart.
The axe lifts over Fotheringay. A soft
wind from the north touches her cheek as she climbs
the steps to the scaffold. There is no
answer, she thinks, and no beginning. But where
is all this smoke coming from,
blowing into her eyes? She can't see, not even the block.
"In my end is my beginning."
The axe answers all of her questions.
Wind ruffles the hair of her head as it falls.

Dreams Upon the Sea

I am the film, and you are the camera:
can't you see, we are the wedding of light.
See my hand as it shivers out of focus,
my eyes that become the reflection of yours:
reflection within reflection, the silver screen
in some abandoned cinema still showing
the midnight movies of our hearts' content.

Waters of ocean, pillars of tumbling sand.
I am the prophet, and you are the fire:
can't you see, we are the children of God.
Speak out against the speeches of betrayal,
the songs that spin into spirals of silence,
sounds that are muffled in careless echoes
that even escape the directional microphone.
Show me the mercy that you show to strangers,
no questions asked, no alibis invented,
pain in your eyes when they pass on their way.

I am the road, and you are the traveller:
can't you see, we are a journey without end.
Hear the hiss of ten wheels on a road after rain,
the crack of the pebble that scars on your screen:
echo of songs that are hitching a ride,
of a boy in the dust with a Gibson guitar.
My ticket's on track for the moccasin dawn,
footsteps trip over the east edge of night.

Or: I am the word, and you are the breath:
can't you see, we are the poem of our lives.
Remember the books on our brick-and-board shelves,
the ones we will never have time to re-read;
sound of a sigh when you open the pages

of poems whose lines are the measure of love. Tonight
my house is surrounded by wings, and we
own nothing of the sky except its name—
name of the nameless, name of the Song of Songs.

Between the Windows of the Sea

"And then went down to the ship"—Odysseus,
the 20th century wanderer, weaver of words
(words with two meanings), coiner of names
that turn out to name No One—Odysseus,
are you lonesome tonight? have you already
used up all the addresses in your epic black book?
For once in your wandering, are there no nymphs
to straighten the curls in your blue-black beard,
get ready for your second coming? Odysseus,
the wine-dark sea's been breathalysed, and soon your
ship will be impounded, you will be declared
"confused," or some such weasel word, and No One
will be found guilty, drunk at the wheel,
not someone to be (like Circe) lightly tossed aside.
Be patient; be prudent; Ezra Pound at least has
understood your predicament. And in translation
(when you're most vulnerable) your words—
they're "yours," you know, only on loan—will still be
spoken, albeit in an Anglican accent, "in officina Wecheli,"
for the benefit of those who never saw you sail.
The last thing you remember, before you stripped and kneeled:
chains of memory, chains of association, chains
of bronze, of lead, of Iron-Age iron.
The sea will be your ultimate mistress, the wine-dark
sea will be your witness, and I (I warn you), I
will be your mutineer.
Have the brachycephalic Aegean cops
busted your ass once too often? What,
in the name of Poseidon, do you think you're playing at?
The various voice of Polyphemus calls you,
night is approaching, the sheep are herded home,
and another of your crew goes down his gullet.
Will you be next, Odysseus, will No One

be dashed to the ground, consumed, and never
buried at home, in the forgotten soil of Ithaca?
At night sometimes you dream of those digested men:
the Viennese doctor could never get to the
bottom of that one. But then you lied to him—
of course. That's what No Man does, isn't it, Odysseus?
The lights go out in one more western town.
Ocean reaches her slim pale arms towards the horizon.

My Back Pages

I was the Dauphin of France, and she
was Madame Guillotine. It was 1791,
so I had to take precautions, there was
much to look out for if I wanted to grow
older in her company. I became Marat,
then I was Danton, and now I think
I'm Robespierre—tactical incarnations,
younger each time, but never younger
than her. The clean bright blade
that rises in the morning sunlight, falls
now—as the crowd historically sighs.

Six White Horses

To the lovers; to the abandoned lovers; to those who always
live alone in furnished rooms, outside the gates, or
outside the gospel—these words.
The machinery of justice is not concerned for you;
law students learn your lives as textbook arguments;
you are always found guilty. Already you know what
must happen next: one morning there will
be someone beside you saying "I love you,
honest I do," but you know that's not true, don't you?
I'm only rehearsing your life again, repeating what you
know and have always known. You turn to them,
you ask if their love is for real, for good, for
always, like it is in the movies. And they
say Yes, honest, the world will come to an end, or
that'll be the day. But you will be alone,
you will be abandoned. In the end you can only
agree with the verdict, fall in love with the jury.
So you turn in your bed, to the rumpled pillows
where someone slept last night, and find only a goodbye note—
are you glad? Did you see that one coming?
You're alone again, like some king or queen
tonight in exile, on the way to a famous execution.
Sweet thing, you whisper, dear dead sweet thing.
Marie Antoinette, perhaps, or the Archduke Ferdinand.

Trouble

And love survives, a rabbit in a hat—
now you see it, now you don't—
the magician's hand is on his
heart is on his sleeve, but the vanished rabbit
is alive, somewhere, as tough as love and
filled with longing for the light.

>   With all my love, he says; with all my kind regards.
>   Gold chains are fastened round his ankles
>   as if he was working some road-gang of desire.
>   If today was not an endless highway, he sings, and
>   it sounds so familiar, you've read that his voice
>   was convicted of passion, but is out on parole.

A member of the audience empties his volunteer
purse (and his heart) on the table beside the empty hat.
But the rabbit is still in hiding, and then
"Oh!" the magician exclaims, sifting the coins,
"what have we here? A rabbit's foot."

>   Kind regards don't mean that much to those convicted
>   of crimes against the state, against the heart.
>   Love chooses to stay in jail, in hiding; love
>   is the last resort, can't show its hand too soon.

This is what the rabbit remembers: a midnight field
which lovers walk through, as the magic moon
goes proudly through its phases, disappearing
from time to time, like coins from an audience purse.
Bad luck to keep a good-luck charm, the rabbit thinks:
to believe you can cut up love, yet keep it whole.
Worse even than waiting, helpless, inside a tall black hat.

Idiot Wind

I've been out in that wind too long,
waited too long for what it never could give me:
for something politics never could give me, or even
you never could give me. I've spent my life waiting
on railway platforms at 3 AM, stubbornly watching
the notice boards tell me which trains are no longer
running on time: Hamburg: Berlin: the same dark cities, the same
boards announcing cancellations, missed connections,
near collisions. And other lives I've wasted in
the drab, sad rooms where commercial bodies
sigh, press themselves against each other, simulate
trees of life, or trees of forbidden knowledge,
while all the time the wind could tell you there is nothing there
the paying customers do not already know—
springtime in Paris, dreamtime in Alexandria, all these illusions
turned into rogue computer viruses
slowly spreading through the Internet, forcing their way
into whatever still gives me memories of vacant pleasure:
autumn leaves, smoke drifting into grey November air.

Subterranean Homesick Blues

If only the night had a name of its own.
I am not the name that I sign to my name.
Could you lend me eleven dollars until next Wednesday?

Only the sad and the lonely read footnotes.
Turn your frog pond into a gold mine.
Back in the 60s, poems were hard currency.

The world has been silent since the Romans left.
Clock makers always take their time.
To live outside the law you must be honest.

When is the plane leaving for Ho Chi Minh City?
God is a humorist, that's why He's unemployed.
And before we could catch our breath, it was 1970.

Her voice broke into the glass like an artificial waterfall.
Were you ever a member of the Weathermen?
Born in Poland, now resident in Tadzhikistan.

Come with me to the airport, you can take a taxi back.
In 1968 I was twenty-four years old.
She spent her final years alone on the Rue Christine.

    Said the joker to the thief.
    I'll be your San Anton Rose.
    Give me a break.

You don't remember the way I used to play golf.
Shelter your eyes from the total eclipse.
From Edmonton to Victoria I watered the jade.

    The poem begins before the commercial ends.
    Storm clouds gather over the Straits of Juan de Fuca.

In the Alleyway, with his Pointed Shoes and his Bells

Peace to all those who read his bones.
Will Shakspear, late of Stratford,
come into London and into his own:
with his narrow almond eyes, that gleam
tranquility and secrets, the masochism
and the greed of genius. There is a cryptic
splendour in those eyes' sharp margins:
on alert, on demand, letting nothing escape
the mesh of their retinal screen. A hawk
wheels in the thin smudged London sky:
of course it is a metaphor, it is steel, it is
fire. It is already a line of dialogue,
but Hamlet doesn't know that yet. Meanwhile,
Will is in the tavern drinking with the players.
"Bring us another ale!" is the cue for this scene—
us drinkers, us actors, us workers in song—
no star system here, one extra pint is the playwright's
reward for all the golden lines he gives them. Later,
when the moon comes up, yellow with harvest,
her shivering light spills over his manuscripts:
false-hearted lovers, treacherous intriguers,
idols of intellect and vanity, fools, one and all
fall to the poisoned sword, the devious plot,
and the demands of his poetry. The writer is always
cruel, detached, a complicitous servant of
death and perfection. Shakspear in secret
surrenders to every suspected emotion
with such abandon that the audience holds
its breath in balance. On the stage,
pale shadow of himself, Will plays his part:
ghost on the battlements, ghost at dawn
retreating into torment, leaving his son suspended
between cancerous love and ecstatic despair: between

the insupportable cry for revenge—this
king must die / long live this king—
and the frozen mist that creeps into his soul.
The fever's on him now: he sees the schizophrenic
queen; he lives her death; he sees his prince
of time and hesitation break upon his wheel:
swords and poison, pen and parchment, acts and images of Will.

The Harder Stuff

Never trust a man who wears dark glasses indoors.
"Could you give me a hand?" he asks, and you will
learn from experience, he means an arm and a leg.
"To us!" he says, raising a glass of Burgundy:
"drink to our future happiness!" and you should know
that isn't a good year, that's your life
blood he's rolling over his tongue. So what if he sings
and writes you romantic poems: all the more reason to
call in the cops, haul out his wallet, check his ID.
It doesn't say "poet" on his driver's license, does it?
Wine may improve with age in a cool dark place, but
never trust a man who wears dark glasses indoors.
"Could you give me your heart?" he asks, and you will
learn from experience, he means that literally.
"To us!" he says, raising a second glass of Burgundy:
"hold onto your dreams, there's a hurricane coming!"
You wonder what line he'll try next, and what colour his eyes are.
"Love that outfit you're wearing," he murmurs confidentially,
and actually raises his glasses, just for a moment. His eyes are green.
"Call me Ishmael," he whispers, and flips them back down. Too late—
you've seen inside him, you're hooked, you're gone. "This one is
mine," you announce, and lead him by the nose to your optician.

Eternal Circle

You're the one who sang me
"Blowing in the Wind" in 1963:
down the spiral of the windy years
the memory spins like an old LP.
Shaky focus; sound turned low;
street of adolescent dreams.
You're the one who started me
hearing the way words go out dancing,
my echoes answering the wild
heart rhythms of your songs, the hard rock
beat and electric pulse, and a prairie storm
in that high winding organ,
the sting of guitars. You put me on
record, on notice, on edge: I was
breaking the rules, I was leaving home.
Heat of summer in St Andrews
where "my friends and I spent many an afternoon":
we were freewheeling in your footsteps, we
were blowing in your wind, we were dying, dead,
born into new kaleidoscopes of light.
In the devious streets of memory,
time stands at attention to your voice.

The Anaesthetist's Question

So tell me about Canadian
poetry, sd the anaesthetist, do we
have any authors that
measure up? And I

was wondering how to answer, when
the sentence in my head just
stopped. And something slid
into my veins, the end of it

all, until three hours later.
Meanwhile the surgeon
punctured me with two holes
and in one inserted a tele-

vision camera. Imagine that:
at last I'm on TV, or
TV is on me. *In* me. A picture
transmitted back to my

outside world. Guiding the instruments
stitching, stapling together
the torn parts of me. In living
colour, as I lay

expensively on that bed.
Later I'm back, I'm waiting for
my body to begin again,
and I resume

the anaesthetist's question: do we have poets
that measure up? to what? to what
the surgeon did for me
rhyming by remote control

on a TV monitor? making me whole
without remainder, without even
(to my great disappointment) keeping
a videotape? If I could see

inside myself, the microcosm of
my lower abdomen, I'd write you
a Canadian poem, a measured line
would take your breath away

surgeon, anaesthetist, gentle reader
of all my hidden meanings:
unfold me to myself, and let me
stutter in wonder, sing

in patient praise.

Alberta Mornings with Vicki and Gail

Waking into winter dawn, 20 below
trees in their fuzz of white frost
the whole white sky
cracking over the house
into the clarity of cold

Driving the Sherwood Park freeway
swirl of snow across the surface
trusting to a grip of wheels
on the hard, reluctant ground

And playing the radio, CBC
Alberta mornings with Vicki and Gail

Refineries off to the north
Manhattan in miniature
lights on the skeleton towers
and clouds in the air of
frozen exhaust

Driving into Edmonton
82nd Avenue at 8 AM
passing the banks of Bonnie Doon
the railway tracks of old Strathcona

And playing the radio, CBC
Alberta mornings with Vicki and Gail

Back in the days before Ralph Klein
before the selling of Wayne Gretzky
when ceegar-chewing dumpy old Tom Wilkinson
still quarterbacked the Eskimoes

Back in the days when Edmonton
looked down its civic nose at Calgary
back in the days when nobody
ever thought that anybody
could be nostalgic for the 1970s

And playing the radio, CBC
Alberta mornings with Vicki and Gail

Crossing 109th Street
through the decaying remains of Garneau
attaching my car to a block-heater plug
that prairie winter's umbilical

Sitting in the parking lot a moment
to hear the end of an interview
Gail's gentle voice, or the sudden
cackle of Vicki's laughter
so much like Janis at the end
of her own, of her own last song

Then turning off the radio, CBC
Alberta mornings with Vicki and Gail

Alberta mornings with Vicki and Gail

Willow

(1)
Denmark, they say, is a cold country.
On the day I was born, they say, a storm
rode in from the Baltic: ice and sleet
shrouding the walls of Elsinore, the wind
howling at the windows where my mother
bore me, and died. That is what they say,
what they all say. I have no voice.
My brother and father speak for me,
even in my private letters
they sign my name. I am silent
and alone in this cold country, I do not
question why it is that sometimes
I feel warm.

(2)
They taught me to weave tapestry, a
modest pursuit. I sit here for hours
in the winter light, weaving my mother,
weaving her face into every vision. Of course
my father would not like it if he saw
(though he never sees) her face in my patterns:
so I must give her a disguise. She is a bird,
she sits on the branch of a tree, over-
hanging a river. Like me, she has no voice.
She sits in the willow and weeps
and I touch her face each evening as I leave
her silent room.

(3)
My brother and I are commanded
to play with the prince. He is the same

age as I am, and sometimes I feel
sorry for him. He has no brother;
he has no sister. His father is always
off somewhere fighting silly wars.
All he has are servants, courtiers:
they comb his hair and show him his face
in smiling mirrors. He and my brother
fight each other with wooden swords;
my brother knows that the prince must always win.
Or else the prince politely tries
to play with me: but he doesn't know how.
No one knows how. Sometimes I think
I am not even here, I am already
with my mother
in the tapestry.

(4)
This morning my brother
is proud, he says
my father has become
the most important
man in Denmark, short
of the king himself.
My father is now
the king's most high
and trusted councillor,
I think
has the king ever heard
my father in the deep
dark of the night
when he weeps,
remembering my mother?
when he weeps and weeps,
remembering my birth?

(5)
My father speaks for the king.
My brother speaks for me.
The prince speaks for himself: that is
what it means to be a prince.
As usual, I speak for no one.

Unless:
yes, let me speak for the willow,
let me speak for that green bending tree
by the bank of the river that runs
outside the walls
of this grey castle, else no more.

Let me speak for its silver leaves
as they bend like courtiers to touch
their foreheads to the flowing water.

(6)
The prince is leaving the castle,
leaving Denmark. I did not imagine
such a thing was possible.
He will be a student in Germany
at a place called Wittenberg
so far to the south that I think
the sun must never set there.

Before he left he gave me a ring
and asked me to wear it for him
until he returns. Of course I do not dare
to place it on my finger:
I looped it on a silver chain, which
was my mother's,
and I wear it around my neck
under my dress,
where only my mother can see.

(7)
And if I should say, I love
him, the prince, my
father and my brother say
do not
believe him, he is far
beyond your star, oh
sister, daughter
cast him far
beyond your thoughts, this
must not be, and if
I should say

I should say, but I have
no voice, I must wait
for the prince himself
to speak for me
the words of declaration, words
to set my own tongue free,
as he would, oh
willow tree
believe it, as he would
were he not far
in Wittenberg, were he

not far from me
where I sit by the willow waiting
watching this river
flow, northward, away from me
away from the prince, and into
the shivering sea.

(8)
Consider my dream
ladies, sweet ladies, tell me
how strange is my dream:

that the king
is dead, and his
brother rules

that my father
is dead, and his
killer lives

that my lover
is mad, and his
shadow still

lives to attack me
with words like
poisoned swords:

sweet ladies, tell me
if all
these things be done:

then how shall I
my true love know
from the other one?

By his cockle hat and staff,
lady,
by his sandal shoon.

Camille Claudel

            entered the long
night of her interment night
of burial in memory Camille
Claudel inscribed so many now a name
on a plaque on a grey stone
wall grey trees grey morning
waters of the Seine beside the narrow
street along the margins of
the silent island Quai
d'Anjou where as I pass
a furniture van unloading swings
from an upper storey sofas descending
like puppets on ropes and the road
is blocked until two workmen bodily lift
a car out of its parking space a bus
of impassive tourists squeezes by
the wooden doorway 27
where Robert McAlmon in perpetual rage
ran Contact Editions from the basement where
no plaque remains Camille is straying
down with her dark hair long while Marguerite
Duras in a faint last voice is whispering
C'est tout that's all it's
over and is everything
there is McAlmon rides
the dangling sofa down on the grey
Ile St Louis morning as Camille
longs for longing for escape
carved into stone remembering the day
when careless covered in sculptor's dust
she entered the long

Rue des Archives

                a city of closed doors
you never enter easily these massive
wooden portals on the street with electronic
keypad controls on the locks don't open
no matter how long you wait or live here
needing to know the entry codes
the names of salons inner
circles of power but sometimes like
this morning I was walking through
the Marais looking for the guidebook
mansions the Hôtel de Rohan its
sun's bright horses springing strong
out of a blank stone wall I passed
a door was standing open on
Rue des Archives I looked inside
austere and classical courtyard beyond
the doors and other doors and "French"
windows which are also doors a woman passing
stopped abruptly and like me
looked in and shook her head and commented
ten years I've been walking
down this street each day I've never
seen inside and so she looked
at windows doors inside the courtyard
one moment briefly nodded her head as if
something at last was satisfactory
in Paris you have to take your chance whenever
the closed doors open

for Djuna Barnes

     in the shadow of St Sulpice
within an atmosphere of candles burning
devotion to the Virgin of the bright
Café de la Mairie du Sixième the warm
interior space of October morning ordering
une grande crème un croissant which crowd
my diary on the table top I'm writing
my dreams of yesterday this morning and a young
woman next to me suddenly tumbles
out of her chair a splintered crash
of coffee cups to the floor beside her
pale face dead white dead faint away the
waiters run to help her with
smelling salts and anxious questions I see
small bandage at her elbow given blood
came for a coffee to recover and yet still
doesn't know much of where she is her head
is drooping still she pulls herself awake
gets up unsteadily there is no doctor
to call as once this café might have called
Matthew O'Connor out of pages
of Djuna or of Buffy might have called
to come across the pious square to come
from Hotel Récamier the scene
is famous and is over she is gone
this simple autumn morning coffee
on her table still untouched and
wandering perhaps through nightwood streets
table reset I still return
within an atmosphere of candles burning
my diary in this October morning
bloodless fainting shallow pale
of St Sulpice

The Artist's Confession
(translated from Charles Baudelaire)

Autumn
days ending early
cut through

cut till it hurts

Moments you seek out and savour
though you can't define them
you want to feel

that sharp edge
going on forever

let your eyes drown
in that long delight
of sky and ocean

silent and alone in all
that deep and virgin blue

A small sail shudders in the wind
on the edge of sight
and you accept it as an image of yourself
how small and isolated is this life
you can't get out of

and the waves break on the beach
repeating like a one-note song

How quickly in a dream
identity slips away:
you're thinking the world

and the world is thinking you

but these thoughts weave like music
flash like images:
they don't quibble on points of logic
or work out syllogisms

And somewhere in here it all
gets to be too much for you
whether it's you projecting out
or the world invading in
it's too much

the energy overflows

you can't contain it all in pleasure
and the excess
begins to disturb you
begins to torture you

your nerves are strung tense
and out of tune

Now the depth of the sky
does nothing but perplex you
its clarity angers you

and the goddamn sea
doesn't give a damn about you:
it just goes on and on
being the sea
being the goddamn sea

Doesn't it always end this way? beauty
brings pain and you have to
run like hell away from it

And that cold bitch, Nature, she's
always the one that wins in the end

why can't she leave you alone
stop leading you on
with your own
desire and pride?

You want to study beauty
but it's a fight to the death
and being an artist means only
that you get to cry out
one time before you lose

Dusk

(translated from Pierre Reverdy)

As evening falls the
cat's eyes open.

Beside a window we
sit together, watching and

listening to all that is
nowhere else

but in ourselves. At the end
of the street is a line and

a line above that one: trees, traced
patterns of lace

against the sky. Oh
city, city

where have you disappeared
drowned in the depth

of water, dusk,
and a cloudy sky?

J'ai tant rêvé de toi
(*translated from Robert Desnos*)

I've dreamed so much about you
that you're no longer real

Is there still time
for me to touch your living body
kiss your mouth
kiss there the birth of your voice
that voice I adore?

I've dreamed so much about you
my arms are so used to enclosing
only myself when I think they're enclosing
your shadow
that now perhaps they can never
trace the outline
of your real body

And perhaps
if I were faced with a true apparition
of all that has haunted and ruled me
these days and years
I would myself, no perhaps about it,
become a shadow

All these careful
calculations of feeling!

I've dreamed so much about you
high time that I woke up
I'm asleep on my feet
my body's exposed
to all the simulacra of life and love

and you
the only thing I can count on, I can't
even touch your brow
your lips
any more than I could the first strange face
I met on the street

I've dreamed so much about you
walked so much
talked so much
I've slept so often with your ghost
that now, when all is said and done,
nothing is left for me
but to become a ghost among the other ghosts
a shadow a hundred times more shadowy
than the shadow that walks
and will walk, softly
across the sundial of your life

sur le cadran solaire de ta vie

Sourin

for Ian Hamilton Finlay

At Sourin the road runs straight
uphill into mist

I'm driving round Rousay
the wrong way, heading for

the great ship of death

Over the hill the mist thins out
on the shore of Sariskaill Bay

nothing to the north but Westray
and Papa Westray

a few rocks, skerries, cliffs

where seabirds throng
spectators on a terracing

Twelve compartments in the Midhowe Cairn
twelve on each side

the bones lie scattered or crouched
cold in their boat of stone

The grave mounds cling to the hillside
above Eynhallow Sound

sheep graze obstinately, chewing
five thousand years of damp grass

I stop at a phonebox and call Ian
OK, I tell him, I'm on Rousay
where do I go next?

To Sourin, where I've already been
To Sourin, where the road runs straight

uphill into mist

Uckermunde

for Hartmut Lutz

In graveyards there are always stories
those minimal narratives
of birth and death

> Anna Lutz
> 1875-1966

She was a little crazy at the end, says Hartmut
crawled out her window in her nightgown
onto the neighbour's roof
(later he shows me the roof)
but happy, he says, happily crazy

In graveyards there are always stories
a woman walking onto ice
she thought she had an infectious disease
told her children not to come near her, and
no one believed her, till
the ice believed her

> (I have my stories too
> searching for my grandfather's
> strangely neglected grave
> the toppled headstone)

Hartmut on a winter's day in Rensburg
searching for a grave he'd promised to find
of a man he never knew
a man who drank herbicide
and died, a refugee
while the swing bridge over the Kiel Canal
stood open against the hospital
on the further shore

We get back into the Trabi
it coughs to life
All these stories, says Hartmut, all these sad stories
we should tell some happy ones
Tell me how you met Ruth, I suggest
and that story lasts us
all the way home
to Bömitz

Protection

When I moved out of the safe
family-approved boarding-house
and ended up in my final year on Abbey Street
with a grim-faced landlady who served
Scotch Eggs every Wednesday, without fail
protected by thick layers of batter:

I slept in an inner room, and every night
to get to it I had to pass through Bill's
—which wasn't often a problem, usually
he was blissfully unconscious, sleeping the sleep
of the practiced drunk, or else he was out
getting that way:

Bill Horsburgh. In all my sheltered life
I'd never met anyone so crude, so gentle,
so much a mixture of everything I was not.

He had long, Beatles-mop hair (in
1964), and a big nose, and quiet eyes.
He had no local girlfriend, but at weekends
went off to various cities (Dundee, Edinburgh), returning
with lurid Monday morning stories he no doubt enjoyed
shocking me with. He told me that he always
refused to wear a rubber, making his women
accept him as he demanded, with no protection.
I listened with both credulity
and incredulity.
                    (I was still a virgin
and the woman I hopelessly loved
lived just a hundred yards away, around the corner
of Greenside Place. I was writing
romantic poems of contented despair, while Bill
was screwing half of Scotland, without condoms.)

At other times he would instruct me
on the delights of a cheap drunk: why two
bottles of rotgut were better than one
quality vintage. With a typologist's precision
he catalogued degrees of drunkenness
from "paralytic" through to "neutered."
One night I asked him to protect me
when I went to the local pub, drank two
pints of beer and three fast whiskys
then staggered home and tried to write
a poem from my liberated consciousness—
nothing doing.

But Bill sat with me, smiled, and saw me through,
made sure I didn't vomit, got cleanly to bed
in the inner room. I never saw him angry, never heard
a mean or vicious word from him. Whatever it was
he was supposed to be studying, I never
saw him do any work. He read Anaïs Nin
and not much else. At the end of the year
he slipped out of my life, as if on his way to another
sexual weekend. I have never
heard from him again so much as a whisper,
a breath in the night from the outside room
where he lay, neutered, in some distant dream
my memory has left me of him,
unprotected.

Canto One

(1)

And then went down to the ship,
which was waiting by the shore, which had been
always waiting: as there is always

someone waiting, paid by the hour, for the hero
to wind up his epic similes, and then
go down to the ship, go down

to the underworld and back again, which is
not a retum trip usually made
by the rest of the crew, waiting, unpaid by the hour

along the shore where an endless blue
stretches across a Greek afternoon, that clarity
of skies and tides and circling birds

and the hero's eyes like sunset, going down.

(2)

Lie quiet Divus by the Seine embankment
in the shadow of the great cathedral, Mary's
dappled robe of chestnut branches:

a battered metal cover, *bouquiniste,*
the dealer dreamily assessing
potential customers: this one's American

it seems, red hair, red beard, and a green
silk jacket has seen better days, not likely
to buy a book of mediaeval Latin

surely? but his eye's on fire,
his hair is streaming in Our Lady's sky,
and that beard juts out into the river's wind

and then

      went down

            to the ship

Oral Examination

Saw me coming
did you?

Kept it all in
to yourself?

Went out on a
broken limb?

Played the fool nowhere
but in your own house?

Let your right hand know
what it's doing?

Gone to see a man
about a dog?

Let the sun go
down on your wrath?

    Seen the light?

    Gone to blazes?

    Given a damn?

Lampman's Heart

strained, rheumatic, straining
always one portage beyond

(and in the distance, Ottawa
city of closing doors and piling paper)

wanting to drain the heat
like a reservoir for temporary life

shoreline, gravel, boulder, scrabble up
over the height between two slates of lake

the sky a grey like parchment, civil laws
to regulate the yearning of the heart

broken, murmured, spread like rumour's breath
into the poems he would never write

November sunlight, cold in the clearing's damaged eye
blind light, dead sun, the heart's beat failing

the withered edge of all he could not see
but listened to, in the stuttered strain

of the last portage, in the waterlogged
and fatal (parchment) skin of a red canoe

Tucson Library

No ideas but in
weapons. And no reading
allowed. You are all
in limbo. Only the
library exists.

Angelica stands by the sea

Angelica stands by the sea
where the grains of the sand are as clear
as wine in an Imagist poem

Angelica stands by the sea
though some say it has never stood by her
she is lost in the waves' small catalogue

Angelica stands by the sea
and the small boys watch her from the dunes
scribbling in their sketchbooks

Angelica stands by the sea
and searches the horizon for a sail
—öd' und leer das Meer

Angelica stands by the sea
and the tide comes lapping round her ankles
as if she had stepped through glass

Angelica stands by the sea
the sea wind whispering around her body
my dear and ah! my dear

Angelica stands by the sea
and I have turned my face
(my bitter face)   inland

Things are better in Milan

Things are better in Milan
Things are a lot better in Milan
You loved me in the morning in Milan
Your kisses in Milan tasted like late summer wine
Your scarf was a psalm for the wind in Milan
In Milan my words came alive on the page
I found a shop in Milan that sold delicious olives
I won the weekly Milanese lottery
The Milan newspapers called me a genius
Even the weather in Milan was always perfect
In Milan I arranged for the assassination of two particularly odious
world leaders who had long oppressed their people and stood in
    the way of peace
I knew that I would always love you in Milan
There was a cyber café in Milan where for the price of a cup of
espresso I could transmit my poems to every e-mail address in
    the world
I knew that there was no death in Milan

So of course I came to Venice, to its fading mansions, to its flood-
ing piazzas, to its rotting foundations, to its sinking palaces, to its
overpriced gondolas, to its long and losing battle with the sea

I had to leave Milan
I just had to leave Milan

I've seen some lonely history

I've seen some lonely history
shivering in the cold
of Paris November streets

snow on the edge of the embankment
along the Ile Saint Louis
history between the branches glancing

over to Notre Dame and the bunkered
gates of the Deportation Memorial
jagged iron on the divided river

and history lonely as always
repeats the names of the dead
stands there for days repeating them

as November falls into December
the Christmas lights go on
organ music fills the rose

while an old clochard with a bottle at his lips
repeats the names of the dead
like a shadow on the sundial of your life

—*sur le cadran solaire de ta vie*
oh elegant dark ghost
keeping some kind of record

at the gunpoint of history

My skin is made of stars

My skin is made of stars
I want you to be my astronomer

Gentil Rousseau

(1)

Gentil Rousseau tu nous entends
Nous te saluons
Delaunay sa femme Monsieur Quéval et moi
Laisse passer nos bagages en franchise à la porte du ciel
Nous t'apporterons des pinceaux des couleurs des toiles
Afin que tes loisirs sacrés dans la lumière réelle
Tu les consacres à peindre comme tu tiras mon portrait
La face des étoiles

(2)

Gentle Rousseau you hear us
We salute you
Delaunay his wife Monsieur Quéval and me
Let our baggage pass without duty at heaven's gate
We will bring you brushes, colours, canvases
So that, in your holy retirement, in that true light
You may devote your hours to painting, as once you drew my portrait,
The face of the stars

(3)

My dearest, gentle, sad Rousseau
I hope you hear us now
As we sing your praises
Robert and Sonia, the rider, and me
We're on our way to heaven
Don't give us a hard time getting in, old gatekeeper
We'll bring you brushes, paints, canvases, whatever you need
To spend those blessed easy hours
In the light that tells no lies

Painting, nothing but painting
With the same devotion you gave once to my portrait
The face of the stars

(4)
Sweet, lost Rousseau
All your friends are here to praise you
"Delaunay sa femme Monsieur Quéval et moi"
These are our payments at the pearly gates
Let us in for free
We're bringing you a lifetime of supplies
You must spend eternity painting
Here in the real light
(My portrait was only the model)
The smiling stars

(5)
Are you on e-mail at last
Gentle Rousseau?
Here's Robert, here's Sonia, here's me:
apollinaire@stgermain.com
When our bags get x-rayed in Seattle
Turn a blind eye to the bootleg discs
MacDraw, pirated MacPaint
In virtual space you have limitless band-width
And cyber-light
As once you downloaded a file of my face
To write a program for
The software of the stars

(6)
Rousseau
Salute
Delaunay
Heaven
Colours
Light
Portrait
Stars

(7)
Rousseau you're famous now
People write books in your praise
Quote what Delaunay and I once said about you
All of us call you the customs-agent of heaven
All of us want to pass through
And join you in that real light
All of us want you to paint our portrait
Since now you possess eternity—
Rousseau
Face it, you've become a star

(8)
Gentle Rousseau, listen
We are all one now
The painters, the poets
All dead
All gone to heaven
There are no barriers, Rousseau
No need for customs agents
We can paint in pure light
Write poems without words
Again you will draw my portrait
And my face, like your face, will become
The face of the stars

(9)
A bas Guillaume! Apollinaire
We salute you
Stephen Scobie, my wife, all my friends
Let my poems pass, be kind in your reviews
I'll bring you paper, ink, and pens
On the street that bears your name in Paris
And if you write, perhaps I can translate
"The Face of the Stars"

For Konrad Gross

Wolf wind, silver wind
high splintering descant wind

hitching a ride off Bornholm
hedging along the Hanseatic coast

Lübeck wind, DDR wind
wind demanding passports at the border

Kiel wind, Baltic wind
following wind when you set to sea

wind in your face as you turn to the North
wind that sings to the seeds of your memory

wind of all the wise words you have spoken
veering wind of all your passing years

sliding down the tongue of the Kieler Förde
spilling from the contours of your sail

Letter to Heather: On the Line

Dear Heather,

What can I say about the line? The line
returns, always, to its starting point: it is
a question of margins, marginality,
where the line ends
it begins. It comes back like a ghost
haunting our breath. It dies a long death
on its search for the right hand margin
and then is born again. Revenant, Resurrectionist—
the line is all we have
we have to live by. Our lives on the line.

But is that what you meant? The poetic line?
or that primal mark, hand to paper
(sand, canvas, wall, stone: blank surface)
first gesture of inscription
already dividing space, giving figure and ground,
line of a face in profile, line
of trees on a distant horizon?

We walk the line, we draw the line,
sometimes we cross the line. It is a sign
(a lyin' sign) for limit and transgression.
"Oh you see that line that's movin' through the station"—
we line 'em up and shoot 'em down.
The line starts here.

Heather, my favourite line is still the coast:
long stutter of islands and inlets
and on a particular beach, a shifting line
moving to some
equation: where the tide

advances and returns
across the level slip of sand.
I want a line as slow as that, twice-daily pulse,
or the breath-line pausing, reaching out
and coming home. Dear sweet familiar ghost
on the margin once again.

Stephen

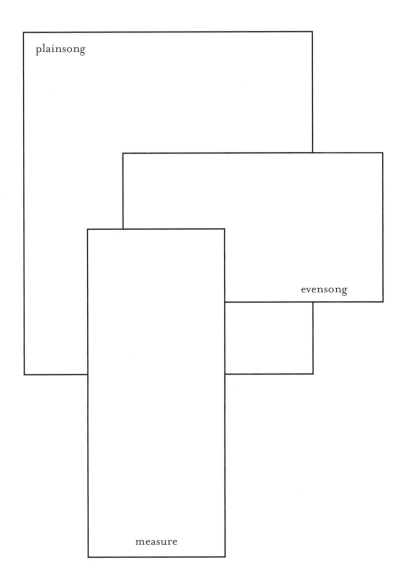

plainsong

evensong

measure

Bar Goya

Sitting in a bar in Madrid with
a martini and far too much
light

my cell phone rings, I
answer it, a voice, it's
Goya speaking

The call seems urgent, he screams
and grunts a lot, it
sounds like one of Saturn's children on

his way down Daddy's gullet

I guess he misdialled maybe
wanted to speak to Velasquez
there's nothing I can do

but cut the connection, tuck the phone
away in my briefcase, after all
it's a Spanish night and I

don't speak Spanish

Office Hours

Pardon, pardon, asks the sail
spilling wind
as it turns its back on the bridge
over the Kiel Canal.

What seems large at a distance
probably is. Things
are what they seem more often
than not. To this
clause there are always exceptions.

Thesis proposal, *Kidnapped*:
David Balfour as Enlightenment
structuralist anthropologist;
Alan Breck as Coyote;
develop in two hundred pages
or less.

Trabi bouncing on the cobbled roads
(if you can call them that)
of lost
Pomerania: East Germany
"died in minutes of a new
equilibrium."

Leaning over the lattice
of a New Orleans wrought-iron
balcony, Juliet
watches ruined Romeo
cruise along Bourbon Street
seduced by regrettable possibilities
of survival.

When the earthquake struck, she said,
her whole collection
of music boxes started playing—
        imagine
        the discords, the harmonies
as once
        I stayed in the riverbend apartment
        of a famous novelist who
        collected clocks—
assorted chimes on every hour
not quite
together.

My fragment of the Berlin Wall
dug out with my own hands
I keep it
in a small film canister
as if it might yet
develop.

I couldn't wait for Spring.
I had to jump ahead
a dozen time zones
and watch the crocus open gold.

Met you on the road
outside Emmaus.
Didn't think you were Jesus.
Years later reflecting
I could have been wrong.

Bryant Park

A sunny morning in Bryant Park, behind the New York Public Library. Jo Davidson's bronze statue of Gertrude Stein, half life size, sits in immovable contemplation. Strange how the small scale does not diminish her, but somehow makes her more familiar, more approachable. Language gathers inside her; her fingers point to the ground.

All round there is freshness and light: the dappled light under the plane trees, sun shining on the green of new spring leaves. Everything peaceful—

—until a sudden squadron of NYPD, cop cars, white vans, blast past in a wail of sirens, rushing east. Then a few more, a couple of minutes later; and five minutes later, more again.

Meanwhile a couple walks by the spot where I'm sitting. The man is tall, lean, black, with a shaved head; the woman is young, white, wearing bright orange pants. They stop close to me, and stand for a while talking; then the man takes one of the park chairs and sits down, while she remains standing. Literally, she's talking over his head. She's smiling, but she seems nervous; her eyes dart everywhere, looking at anything except him.

Suddenly she starts singing, unaccompanied, some Broadway show tune. She has an indifferent voice, but she just stands there, in the middle of the park, taking the song through to a final high note that she can't quite reach.

He remains sitting.

A dog walker, passing, applauds.

And another siren blasts by, heading east, fast, on 42nd Street.

William H. Bonney meets Chateau Margaux 1859

Billy's holed up in
the MacSween house in Lincoln
on the run for
Brady's murder: soon

the house will be on fire, and Billy
tumbling out the back window
buck naked, for his life
but that's

a couple of hours in the future: now
he's raiding MacSween's icebox, looking
for anything to drink, and finds
some bottles that look like wine

though they're marked
"John Chisum: Private Stock"
and then the name
of a fancy French castle he can't

pronounce: marginal, marg
aux: whatever
with his jack-knife
he shovels out the cork and tilts

the bottle to his mouth and takes
a long swig:
it tastes like nothing
then

as the flavours gather
on the edge of his throat
it tastes like everything:
"Jesus! Charlie . . ."

he turns, but Bowdre's
not there, so he settles
down to drink, more
and more slowly

chewing it back on his tongue:
and the wine keeps crackling
like bullets in dry dust
like a Pat Garrett ambush

two hours,
two bottles later he's drunk
when Murphy and Dolan
set fire to the house

and he's out on the street, two
guns in his hands
returning fire,
he's become

a left-handed legend,
Billy the Kid
outlaw, murderer, and almost
a wine connoisseur

For Dorothy McHale

The mountains were always too high for her,
the sky too close. Raised on the prairies,
she carried in her head another space,
another light. Now she is gone

to whatever space remains
beyond the raincoast's closure of mountains
into the light
of her grand-daughter's smile.

Maureen: poems for the weeks of her dying

(1)

My darling it's been far too long
since I did anything as simple
as write a poem of love just for you.

Sometimes it seems it's been easier
to write in praise of a pile
of Parisian stones

than to remember your smile
and your total generosity.
But even when I was sitting alone

in Paris, Saint Germain des Prés,
you were never absent from me.
Whatever I believe

about beauty, about history,
you are involved in it all.
Fount and foundation.

Remember the photograph
I always carry with me: you
at the tip of the Vert Galant

Ile de la Cité, what year was it
1972? It's tattered
and torn from years in my wallet,

the colours faded, the
edges shredded. Last night
I watched as Mary on computer

restored the colours, filled
in the tears. "Reconstructive
surgery," she called it

and my heart was breaking
because reconstructing you
will not be so simple. I have

no simple responses. I'm numb,
I don't even know how to scream
without

observing myself. But I am not
the subject here. It's you
I must remember, cherish, love

more than I've ever done before.
Exactly
like I've always done before.

(2) Victoria General Hospital, North Tower, Room 612

Outside your room, I have to tell you, everything is still
chaos:

the phonecalls I have to make, our many devastated
friends:

plans to make this house's once familiar space
livable, in alien conditions:

the sleep-troubled nights, the intolerable
unanswerable questions:

even the painters at the house, their details, and my goddamn car
not starting:

only
inside this room I am at peace, with you

quietly sitting, holding your hand, and reading aloud
Tristram Shandy—

is it a digression that an eagle
wheels in the sky of your window?—

we have these days, this time together when
I am happy:

how can I say I am happy? but I am
inside

your room, right now, this weekend, oh
my love

my dearest love
I am happy to be with you, and to watch

the clouds
patrol across your perfect sky.

(3)

> "What thou lovest well remains,
>   the rest is dross
> What thou lov'st well shall not be reft from thee
> What thou lov'st well is thy true heritage"
>   (Ezra Pound, Canto LXXXI)

I've always loved these lines
because I believe them; I've always
believed these lines because
I love them. And never more

than tonight, when I read them to you,
the evening sunlight stretching shadows
over the fields beneath your window, where
the swallows swoop and glide—

what you and I love well, what is
our heritage: a seminar
in 1965, Keith Alldritt, and these lines
returning to us now, so many
decades later—

Pound in the Pisan cage,
under indictment of
the relentless sun:
history's loser, and a poet still
fighting his way
to the slow, reluctant, self-condemnation
telling him at last
"Pull down thy vanity, I say, pull down"—

as in this room
we two together
must pull down everything except our love:
all our unspoken plans
for years together, all
our dreamed and undreamed futures, yet

what we love well shall not be reft from us
what we love well will be our heritage

—moments like this, when my voice
speaking these words
hangs in the air between us, surrounds
and pleasures us:

"Palace in smoky light. Troy
but a heap of smouldering boundary stones.
ANAXIFORMINGES! Aurunculeia!"

(4)

I'm looking into your heart:
it's green.

Or at least in this computer
generated image

it's green. Brighter than any
leaf or lime.

It seems like a small pear,
pulsing

77, 78, beats per minute
counted on another screen.

So many times
it beats for you, it

beats for me. I watch the green
image clarify

and I'm in there with you, my
colourless heart

keeping time.

(5)

> "And here's a man
> still working
> for your smile"
>   —Leonard Cohen

So here's a man still working

for your smile,
for your memory,
for your reading of Balzac,

working for your falling hair,
for the times you fall asleep in the middle of a sentence of *Tristram Shandy*,
working for the pillows on your bed,

for the photo albums we go through together,
for the headlines in the morning paper,
for the phonecalls I make to your friends,

working for the view outside your window,
working for the nurses at your side,
working for the sun on a long ago river, Similkameen,

here's a man still working for your silence,
for your music,
for your menus,

working for the best lines in Pound's *Cantos*
        "No wind is the king's wind"
        "What thou lovest well remains"
working for a first edition,

for all the times that you remember and I do not,
for a walk through the English Gardens,
for a picnic lunch in the rain in the Bois de Boulogne,

working for a painting by Mark Rothko,
for music by Haydn on solo piano,
for a cat stretching out, as long as a long afternoon,

working for a summer's day,
for a room to hold you,

working for nothing,
working for a song,

here's a man still working
for your love.

(6)

Maureen these days I think I know
the purpose for my life. Somehow

I used to think it was only poetry:
writing

or teaching it. Whatever claim
I'd stake on immortality would be

hammered down into
structures of words. But now

I find it's much more simple.
I'm here just for you, to give you

whatever time we both have, to tend and care
one day at a time, and every day
is a new page in our Collected Works,
a masterpiece. Nothing I've ever done

so subtle, so eloquent

as when each morning waking

I listen for the song
of your returning breath.

(7)

Oh my darling, where is the rain
in your heart tonight? Is it falling

westward, over the low Sooke Hills
into the long Pacific drift

or does it insist
a repetitious pattern on the roof

of the bedroom we shared,
lying together under the sound

of what it means to be West
Coast, the rain

falling in all our hearts, in yours
and mine? Let the world

end, and begin again here:
in the memories which will never leave me

and in the gap
your naming leaves

like the name we sometimes thought
might be there to be found (though it never was)

the name of the nameless rose
blooming in the rain

in the long, slow, West Coast rain
you were waiting for

in your heart,
on the night you died.

(8)

See, oh see, this final photo.
The scarf on her head is a gift
from Smaro. The cat
is Drum, is always Drum.
Who knows how many times before
she'd read *Orlando*? The light
falls from the window beside her bed.
That was her favourite blouse, her
favourite pillow. Her face
now seems to me reduced, stripped down
to the essentials: her beauty,
her absolute beauty, as it would be
last time I ever saw her, when I said goodbye
and retreated upstairs, allowing
the technicians of death to do their business
and take her
out of my sight, and into
my memory.

(9)

Phyllis, the year is dying, and your
orchid is dying too. The last

purple petals are falling, for all
I can do, I can see

no new points of growth. I remember
early July, those summer days

when Maureen came home from hospital, this
flower was here to greet her, keep her

company through all her dying weeks, orchid
blooming and re-blooming, "deep purple,"

brave bloom on an emaciated stalk. And long after
she died, this presence in the room, lasting

lasting until now, the end of December—
as if it too, like me, can't wait

to be rid of this terrible year.

Notes

This book is a retrospective, chronological selection starting in 1965, and continuing until the end of 2001. It contains only short poems, or poems which can stand alone. Thus, it contains no extracts from book-length narrative poems like *McAlmon's Chinese Opera* (1980), *The Ballad of Isabel Gunn* (1987), *Gospel* (1994), *Taking the Gate* (1996), or *And Forget My Name* (1999). The long sequence "The Dunino Elegies" is represented only by an anomalous "out-take." On the other hand, looser sequences, like *Remains*, *Ghosts*, and *Slowly Into Autumn,* are represented here. One narrative sequence, "Willow," is just short enough to be included in its entirety.

Most of the poems in this selection have been revised for their appearance in this volume. Many of these revisions are slight (a word here, a line there), but some are quite extensive. These notes do not attempt to keep track of the revisions.

"Saint Andrews, 1965"
> Previously unpublished.

"Leaving You My Best Farewell"
"The Black Ponies"
> From *Babylondromat* (privately published, 1966).

"One Word Poems"
> From *One Word Poems* (Lighthouse Press, 1969).

"listen / silent"
> First published as a silkscreen print by Maureen Scobie, 1969. Also appeared in *In the Silence of the Year* (Delta, 1971), and in *Stone Poems* (Talon, 1973).

"The Spaces in Between"
> From *In the Silence of the Year.*

"Naming Mountains"
"Made in USA / Jean-Luc Godard"
"Lenin at the Cabaret Voltaire"
"Word Is"
> From *The Rooms We Are* (Sono Nis, 1974). Despite the publication date, all the poems in this collection were written in 1970-71.

"The Corner of Abbey Street and Greenside Place"
"Bridge-Jumper"
"Saturday Night"
"My Grandmother's Name"
"For Archie Fisher"
From *The Birken Tree* (Tree Frog, 1973).

"Harlequin Acrobat / Arlequin Acrobate"
From *Les toiles n'ont peur de rien* (privately published, 1979).

"The Amateur"
A curiously persistent poem. First written in 1966; revised in 1973; published in 1980 in *in by one, out by four* (Instant Poetry Press, Edmonton); revised again here.

"Black Circle"
"Dumb Animals"
From *Dumb Animals* (League of Canadian Poets, 1980).

"The Children of Photographers"
"West Side Story"
"Fan/atics"
"Songs on the Radio"
"Someday Soon"
"The Wayward Wind"
"Judy Garland"
"A Death in the Family"
"Over Home"
"Cha Till Gu Brath"
"Munich: in the English Gardens"
"mooneow / sooneow"
"Forgetting (l'oubli)"
From *A Grand Memory for Forgetting* (Longspoon, 1981).

"Western Landscapes"
"Molly"
"The Love Song of Alice B. Toklas"
From *The Pirates of Pen's Chance*, co-authored with Douglas Barbour (Coach House Press, 1981). "Western Landscapes" is a word/line acrostic from "Western Wind." "Molly" is a left hand margin reading of the beginning of Molly Bloom's soliloquy; *Ulysses*, Random House edition. "The Love Song of Alice B. Toklas" is a letter/word acrostic from Gertrude Stein's "A Carafe That Is a Blind Glass."

"Rain"
"This Letter in My Father's Hand"
"Poem Beginning with the Line. . . ."
"Cranach"
>From *Expecting Rain* (Oolichan, 1984). "Rain" was also published as a broadside by Peter Quartermain's Slug Press.

"Picasso's Radio"
"The Correction Line"
"Interstate Seattle I 5"
"Lorele/i"
"Housekeeping"
"Fulford Harbour"
"The Disciple's Consciousness"
"Shepherds Abiding"
"Fisherman's Angel"
>From *Dunino* (Signal Editions, 1989). "Shepherds Abiding" was commissioned by CBC radio. In keeping with the principle of not using excerpts from longer works, this selection includes nothing from "The Dunino Elegies," my extended juxtaposition of Rilke and East Fife. But "Fisherman's Angel" was written at the same time (late 1985), and always seemed an orphan adjunct to the longer poem: an "extract" which never quite found its original context.

"Remains"
>From *Remains* (Red Deer Press, 1990).

"Berlin"
"Borders"
"David Livingstone"
"Mirror"
"Mona Lisa"
"Oedipus"
"Rain"
"Telephone"
>From *Ghosts: A Glossary of the Intertext* (Wolsak and Wynn, 1990).

"Horn OK Please"
"The Eyelash of a Camel"
>Previously unpublished. From a visit to India in January, 1992.

"Queen Mary, She's My Friend"
"Dreams Upon the Sea"
"Between the Windows of the Sea"
"My Back Pages"
"Six White Horses"
"Trouble"
"Idiot Wind"
"Subterranean Homesick Blues"
"In the Alleyway, With His Pointed Shoes and His Bells"
"The Harder Stuff"
"Eternal Circle"
>From *Slowly Into Autumn* (privately published, 1995). All the poems in
this collection are word/line acrostics on lines from songs by Bob
Dylan. All the titles are also taken from Dylan songs, though not, in
most cases, the same song as the acrostic base line comes from.

"The Anaesthetist's Question"
"Alberta Mornings with Vicki and Gail"
"Willow"
>From *Willow* (Hawthorne Society, 1995).

"Camille Claudel"
"Rue des Archives"
"For Djuna Barnes"
"The Artist's Confession"
"Dusk"
>From *The City That Dreams* (privately published, 1996).

"J'ai tant rêvé de toi"
Previously unpublished.
These three translations—"The Artist's Confession" (Baudelaire),
"Dusk" (Reverdy), and "J'ai tant rêvé" (Desnos)—are all experiments
in rendering prose poems back into line-division free verse.
Robert Desnos was one of the leading Surrealist poets of the 1920s.
I first came across him in the splendid and vivid portrait of him given
in John Glassco's *Memoirs of Montparnasse*. He lived on the Rue de Seine,
a street replete with small art galleries; and a commemorative plaque
records his address. (In fact, I had always thought his name was
prounced [Dey-noe], until I talked, a few years ago, to an art gallery
owner on the street, who insisted that both the middle and the final S
were pronounced—as in the final S of the Rue de Fleurus, the address
of Gertrude Stein.)
But Desnos was also a Jew. He was denounced to the Nazi authori-

ties and deported, less than six months before the Liberation of Paris in 1944. He was sent to the Nazi concentration camp at Terezin, where he died. His remains were returned to Paris, and the American novelist Kay Boyle records that: "You were not permitted to fulfill the promise as 'one of the hopes of French literature,' but there was one more eternal moment written in the history of that literature when the great and the humble of Paris kneeled in the streets outside St. Germain des Prés (kneeling in homage even on the terrace of the Deux Magots) the day of your funeral, of the burying of the handful of bones that were left, in 1945, of all you were."

Desnos is commemorated now in the Deportation Memorial at the eastern end of the Ile de la Cité, which I have always found to be one of the most moving (and one of the least visited) sites in Paris. The tourist buses for Notre Dame park outside its gates, but how many of the thousands who go to see the glorious rose descend also to pay tribute to the dead of the camps? On the walls of this memorial are carved the concluding lines of what is perhaps the greatest poem by Desnos, which I offer here in humble translation: "J'ai tant rêvé de toi."

"Sourin"
"Ückermunde"
"Canto One"
"Oral Examination"
"Lampman's Heart"
"Tucson Library"
  Previously unpublished; 1996-98.

"Angelica stands by the sea"
"Things are better in Milan"
"I've seen some lonely history"
"My skin is made of stars"
  From *Some Kind of Record*, written March 1999, privately published April 2000. All the poems in this pamphlet begin with a line, or sometimes two lines, which were the opening lines of poems by Leonard Cohen. The pamphlet was published for the Leonard Cohen Event in Montreal, May 2000.

"Gentil Rousseau"
  Paris, 1999. Previously published in *Sources: Revue d'études anglophones* 9 (automne 2000).
  The first poem in this sequence is by Guillaume Apollinaire. It was written in memory of the painter Henri Rousseau, known as the

Douanier, for his occasional employment at a customs barrier outside Paris. Rousseau died in September 1910; a year later Robert Delaunay and Rousseau's landlord, M. Quéval, bought a tombstone for the grave, and Apollinaire wrote these lines on it in chalk. In 1913, the words were chiselled into the stone by Brancusi.

The second poem is a fairly straight, accurate translation (though preserving the not quite accurate English "gentle" for the French "gentil"). Each poem after that takes greater and greater liberties with the original, though never, I hope, entirely losing sight of it.

The final poem recalls the story that Apollinaire, dying in November 1918, heard the crowds outside his window on the Boulevard St Germain calling out imprecations on the German Kaiser Wilhelm, and in his mortal delusion thought that their cry, "à bas Guillaume!," was directed against himself.

"For Konrad Gross"

June 2000. Unpublished, except in a private tribute booklet presented, on his 60th birthday, to Herr Professor Doktor Konrad Gross (Konnie), one of the pioneers of Canadian studies in Germany, and a dear friend for so many years.

"Letter to Heather: On the Line"

From *Line by Line: An Anthology of Canadian Poetry*, edited by and with drawings by Heather Spears (Ekstasis, 2002).

"plainsong"
"Bar Goya"

Previously unpublished. 2000.

"Office Hours"

Privately published, 2001.

"Bryant Park"

Previously unpublished, 2001.

"William H. Bonney Meets Chateau Margaux 1859"

Published in *Zeitschrift für Kanada-Studien*, 2002.

"For Dorothy McHale"
"Maureen: poems for the weeks of her dying"

Previously unpublished, 2001.

STEPHEN SCOBIE was born in Scotland on the last day of 1943, and has lived in Canada since 1965. He gained a PhD from UBC in Vancouver, taught for twelve years at the University of Alberta in Edmonton, and is now a Professor of English at the University of Victoria. As a poet, he has published over twenty books, most of which are represented in this Selection. In 1980, he won the Governor General's Award for Poetry for his book *McAlmon's Chinese Opera*. As a critic, Scobie has published extensively on Canadian literature, including studies of Sheila Watson, Leonard Cohen, and bpNichol. He has also written on topics as diverse as Cubism and Concrete Poetry, Jacques Derrida and Bob Dylan. In 1995, he was elected to the Royal Society of Canada.